THE DOC'S SIDE

The Doc's Side

TALES OF A SUNSHINE COAST DOCTOR

Eric J. Paetkau, MD, FRCS

HARBOUR PUBLISHING

Harbour Publishing Co. Ltd.
P.O. Box 219, Madeira Park, BC, V0N 2H0
www.harbourpublishing.com

All photographs courtesy of the author
Edited by Rosella Leslie and Betty Keller
Printed and bound in Canada

Harbour Publishing acknowledges financial support from the
Government of Canada through the Canada Book Fund and the
Canada Council for the Arts, and from the Province of British
Columbia through the BC Arts Council and the Book Publishing Tax
Credit.

Library and Archives Canada Cataloguing in Publication

Paetkau, Eric J. (Eric Jacob), 1933–
     The doc's side : tales of a Sunshine Coast doctor / by Eric J.
Paetkau.

ISBN 978-1-55017-554-7

     1. Paetkau, Eric J. (Eric Jacob), 1933–. 2. Physicians—British
Columbia—Sunshine Coast—Biography. 3. Medical care—British
Columbia—Sunshine Coast—History—20th century. 4. Sunshine
Coast (B.C.)—Biography.
I. Title.

R464.P335A3 2011   610.92   C2011-904656-3

*To the community in general
and my family in particular*

CONTENTS

The beautiful, rustic setting of St. Mary's hospital in Garden Bay captured my heart.

The End of the Road

It was Sunday afternoon, September 13, 1959, when my wife Bonnie and I came to the end of the gravel road. Before us was a long wooden wharf and the calm blue waters of a bay that was dotted with small islands and bordered by green forested hills. To our left, across a narrow tidal slough, was a large building with a sign that read—rather cheekily, considering that we seemed to be in the middle of nowhere—*Lloyd's Department Store*. Certain that I had taken a wrong turn and become lost, I got out of the car and looked around. There, perched imposingly on a bluff above me, was St. Mary's Hospital.

After three months and 12,000 kilometres of driving across Canada and the United States, Bonnie and I had found what looked to be the perfect country hospital, the place where I would begin my career as a general practitioner/surgeon. We had started our journey in California. I had just completed my surgical internship at the San Diego Mercy Hospital, and after a three-year, long-distance courtship had finally been able to marry the woman I'd fallen for the first day I saw her. Bonnie Johnson was not only intelligent, compassionate and beautiful, she also shared my sense of humour and was willing to travel with me down roads seldom travelled. Our wedding ceremony

The day I became a doctor was an exciting one. Graduation from medical school was conducted with great fanfare and commemorated with a formal portrait.

was held at Ramona's Marriage Place, a romantic adobe building that was built in 1825 for the Estudillo family and later made famous by the Helen Hunt Jackson novel *Ramona* and several movies by the same name. We chose it because we liked the chapel and beautiful gardens filled with climbing roses, geraniums, ornamental fruit trees, vine-covered arbours and fountains.

As we were so far from home and both of us came from families that could not afford to travel, our wedding guests were the friends we had made in San Diego. Among them were many of the people I had worked with, including my mentor, Russ Harbaugh, a bright, practical man and an excellent surgeon. Shortly before our wedding he had offered to finance my surgical residency if I would come back and join his practice.

"No," I said, "I want to be a GP/surgeon somewhere in rural Canada."

"Where will you go?" he asked.

"The first place I come to where I can earn a dollar, because I'm broke."

His response was to lend me $3,000 and admonish me to "look around" before we settled down. Deciding to take his advice and combine our honeymoon with my search for just the right practice, Bonnie and I packed tents and sleeping bags into my year-old Ford Fairlane and headed up the Pacific Coast to British Columbia, a place we both favoured. In Vancouver

I visited the College of Physicians and Surgeons where I presented the registrar with my papers, paid a $200 fee and was instantly registered to practise in this province. Not sure where to start my search, I asked the woman behind the desk for the names of hospitals or clinics that could use a GP/surgeon. She handed me a list of about fifty places, and after looking them over, I said, "Where would you go if you were me?"

"Pender Harbour." She pointed to a listing for a locum that had been posted by a Dr. Al Swan at the Garden Bay Hospital. "It sounds like just the place for you!"

The idea was intriguing, but I had many other opportunities to explore before making a commitment. One of these was a clinic in Burnaby that Bonnie liked. Another was in Kelowna, which I thought would be a good place to settle down. In those days, however, doctoring was still a competitive profession and the manager at the clinic there said flat out, "There's no room for you here. Kelowna has enough doctors."

Young and free of work and responsibility for the first time in either of our lives, we were in no hurry to make a decision. Instead we headed for eastern Canada, camping out and visiting with friends and relatives along the way. Whenever we came upon a place that we liked, we checked with the local clinics for vacancies. One such place was Collingwood, Ontario, but once again I was told, "There's no room here. Move on." It wasn't my style to fight my way into a place where I was not welcome, so we continued our quest, crossing the border into the United States and driving down the eastern seaboard to Miami. Here we parked the car and flew to the Bahamas for the final week of our adventure.

As a wedding gift we had been given a week's stay and one champagne dinner at the Emerald Beach Hotel in Nassau. Of course, by this time we were pretty well broke, and since even coffee at that hotel was fifty cents a cup, we ate the rest of our meals at cheaper establishments. Most of the tourist attractions were also beyond our means, but every morning I would go down to the waterfront and look at the glass-bottomed boats taking people out on trips. And every morning the man in charge would say to me, "Wannah rent a boat, Mistah?"

"No, no," I'd reply. "Just looking."

Finally, after four mornings of this, he asked, "What'sa mattah, Mistah? You on relief?"

"Yeah, you've got it," I answered.

On our last night at the hotel I turned to Bonnie and said, "Well, we're virtually out of money and out of time. I think I'll give Pender Harbour a try."

When she agreed, I placed a person-to-person call to Dr. Alan Swan. I was startled when the man who answered demanded brusquely, "Operator, is this a collect call?" But as soon as she responded that I was paying for it, his unfriendliness vanished. "I'm sorry," he said, "but I've had some bad experiences with guys who've phoned me collect and had me send them $100 for transportation and never showed up."

"Are you still looking for a locum?" I asked.

"Yes, I am." After I described my qualifications, he told me I was hired.

"Okay," I said, "I'm on my way."

We flew back to Florida the next day and headed out right across the USA from the southeast corner to the northwest corner and within a week we were on the Black Ball ferry headed for Langdale. It was a spectacular ferry ride. In our travels we had criss-crossed several mountain ranges, driven past and over lakes and rivers and walked along ocean beaches of every sort, but suddenly here we were on this blue, blue water surrounded by rugged mountains with seagulls screaming overhead, and it just made me feel as if my whole body was swelling up. And the closer we got to the Sunshine Coast, the more I liked what I saw.

After leaving the ferry we drove into the town of Gibsons Landing where we stopped to ask for directions. The first people we asked didn't know of the existence of a hospital.

Then somebody said, "Oh, yeah, there's one up at Pender Harbour . . . I think. You've gotta keep driving."

We followed the road he indicated, a tortuous two-lane highway that seemed to be taking us farther and farther away from civilization because all we could see were trees and more trees. Finally the forest began to give way to a few houses and stores, and on the ocean-side we passed a huge brick building that I learned later was the residential school on the Sechelt Indian Reserve. At the bottom of the little hill just beyond the school we came to a stop sign beside a white and green BC Forestry station where we turned left and followed what seemed to be the main road past some businesses, including a Red and White Store and a police station. Finding no evidence of a hospital here, we parked and went into a place called Parker's Hardware to ask directions once again. We were told to keep on driving.

"When you get to Pender Harbour there's a sign that says:

The gravel road ended unexpectedly right below the hospital and we were there. Gazing out to the bay I thought, "This is my scene."

To Garden Bay. If you go past that sign, you'll end up at the ferry terminal at Earl's Cove."

Wondering what we had got ourselves into, we drove and drove until we found the sign and the turn-off, but now the road was gravel and even more desolate than the highway. Then suddenly the road ended and we were there. Overwhelmed, I gazed up at the twin-peaked, two-storey building with its double row of white verandahs and sunshine glinting off the window panes, and thought, *This is my scene.*

Bonnie and I, newlyweds and fresh arrivals to Garden Bay in September 1959, quickly settled into our new home.

CHAPTER 1

From Russia with Turmoil

I grew up in Rosthern, which lies between the North and South Saskatchewan rivers and is the centre for a farming community that extends nearly fifty kilometres in every direction. In those days the population of about twelve hundred people was primarily Mennonite, secondly Ukrainian and thirdly English. We had a large Mennonite high school called the German English Academy that was also a co-ed boarding school for about a hundred and twenty out-of-town kids.

Except for the butcher, who was a good Catholic Englishman, most of the merchants in Rosthern were General Conference Mennonites who believed in making money and getting an education. Mennonites lived in town, worked at the grain elevators and farmed. Many of them, including my parents, had immigrated from Russia in the 1920s, a time when many members of our Canadian parliament didn't want any more Mennonites because those who had come here in a previous wave had taken up a lot of land and become very successful. But Bishop David Toews, the Moses of the Mennonites, convinced Prime Minister Mackenzie King to allow a second wave, and when Toews could not persuade the Canadian Pacific Railway to finance their transportation outright, he obtained a government guarantee for the loan. It took thirty years for that debt to be repaid and I still remember as a kid in church during the Depression that every fourth Sunday there would be two collections. One was routine, and then they'd pass the plate around for the *reiseschuld* or travel debt. It was a pretty big sum of money, but the community paid it back to the very last penny.[1]

My parents and their friends didn't talk very much about their past, but I did learn some of their history from my maternal grandparents and from a detailed memoir my father wrote during his retirement years. Both came from the eastern Ukraine, which at that time was part of Russia, and grew up in areas that had been colonized in the 1700s by Prussian Mennonites. Lured there with promises of autonomy and religious freedom, the industrious Mennonite pioneers had soon adapted their farming methods to the dry, barren land of the Ukrainian steppes, and over the next hundred years turned Russia into a major exporter of grain to Europe. By 1870 their population had increased to forty-five thousand people and their land holdings to eight hundred thousand acres. By this time, however, tensions between Russia and Germany were causing Czar Alexander II to be concerned about these German nationals who were enjoying special privileges not given to his Russian-Ukrainian peasants. His response was to make Russian the official language in the settlements, establish imperial supervision of the schools, abolish the Mennonites right to govern themselves and deny the military exemption that was crucial to the Mennonites' pacifist beliefs. The Mennonite reaction was to begin a mass emigration from Russia, the first of them leaving for America in 1873.[2]

Faced with the loss of his country's best and most prosperous farmers, the Czar adjusted the military service rule, enabling Mennonites conscripted to the army to perform noncombatant duties such as sanitary service, bridge building and forestry. But under the uneasy truce that followed, the lives of the Mennonites who remained in Russia became increasingly difficult, and their troubles intensified after the unsuccessful 1905 revolution of the Russian peasantry who resented the Mennonites' wealth and privilege.[3]

In the midst of this revolution, my mother, Helen Unger, was born to one of those "privileged" families. She grew up on a huge estate, complete with horses and stables, in the village of New York (now Novgorodskoye), which lies approximately two hundred kilometres east of Chortitza. Her grandfather was the owner and manager of several flour mills and so rich that, when he discovered that there was no school for girls among the Mennonites in New York, he built and initially operated a girls' institute for learning. I was once told that his son, my grandfather Heinrich Unger, lived the life of a gentleman until he was forty, and that my grandmother owned twenty-four place settings of the most expensive china and cutlery you could buy. Only six spoons from those settings were left by the time the Unger family escaped from Russia.[4]

Soon after the onset of World War I in September 1914, the Mennonite farmlands became the battleground where Imperial Russia's Third Army fought the German invaders. Three years later the Russian Revolution and subsequent murder of Czar Alexander and his family brought even more chaos to the region; laws governing the country became non-existent as battles raged between numerous political groups with conflicting ideologies.

By this time my mother was twelve years old and had become a slender, attractive young woman of great courage and intelligence. One day as she was walking home over a small pass from a neighbouring village, she came upon a camp of Cossacks who saw her before she could get away. Wise enough to know what could happen to a girl in such circumstances, she played stupid, picking her nose and wetting her pants; by becoming an target of ridicule instead of a sexual object, she survived.

The Treaty of Brest-Litovsk finally ended this war in March

1918, but more years of internal warfare followed. It was during the Ukrainian revolt (1918–1921, that my mother faced her second near-death experience. Late one night as she was returning home by train from her first year of university in Kiev, the train was held up by bandits and everyone was ordered outside. There was shooting and my mother was scared. Suddenly the woman who was leading the bandits came up to her and asked, "Are you Helen Unger?" Recognizing her as a childhood friend—a Russian orphan girl who had spent many Christmases in the Unger home—my mother said yes. At once the woman shouted, "This one is my prisoner!" She then walked my mother into the darkness and said, "Now run and I'll pretend to shoot you!" Although my mother got safely away, she never went back to university.

While my mother was growing up in relative prosperity, my father, David Paetkau, was not so fortunate. His own father, Henry Paetkau, who was one of a growing number of landless Mennonites, died in 1911 when Dad was just eight years old, leaving behind a widow with nine children and no source of income. The children's care was taken over by two godfathers, and the older ones were sent to live with other families. Dad was sent to the home of a high school teacher in Chortitza who wanted a companion for his son, and although he was supposed to be treated as an equal sibling, in reality his position was closer to that of an unwanted relative.[5]

In his memoirs Dad described his summer holidays when he would return to his home village to work in the fields to help support his mother and siblings. Among his jobs was the task of stooking rye. "The sheaves were scattered all over the fields," he wrote, "and we had to collect them and put them up into stooks of eight to twelve sheaves in such a way as to protect them from staying soaked after a rain . . . The stubble was high, I was barefoot and before you knew it, my shins were scratched up. O, the constant irritation of perpetual scratching against the wounded skin and the washing of sore feet in the evening!"

Two things sustained my father during these hard times. One was his passion for music and the other was his determination to become a teacher. His music training had begun with school choirs supplemented by a few piano lessons that were discontinued when the teacher moved away. After that, Dad used a self-instruction book to teach himself.

When he graduated from the First Classical Gymnasium at the age of fourteen, Dad was informed by his adoptive father that he was no longer welcome in his home. Fortunately, later that summer he learned that his godparents had arranged for him to continue his schooling at the Central School and to board with a distant relative. There he did well academically, but his lessons and his accommodations were frequently interrupted by the revolution.

By the time my father entered the Teachers' Seminary in 1918, the Black Army of Nestor Makhno, a Ukrainian peasant-turned-political leader who was determined to establish an independent Ukraine, was engaged in fighting the German advance into Russia. The peasants regarded Makhno as a hero who attacked the rich and bestowed their property on the poor, but to the Mennonites he was a monster who considered them wealthy German landowners oppressing his Ukrainian brothers. So long as he and his army were around, no Mennonite could be assured of the safety of his life or property. My father wrote that:

On several occasions [Makhno's] appearance scared us to death. And with good reason, too. They massacred every male in the village some twenty miles north of Chortitza. They came to the village and simultaneously several of them entered each house and yard, making sure that escape was impossible, and in cold blood murdered every man and his sons. They did not use firearms, but with sabres and rifle butts hacked and beat their victims to death . . , Makhno pretended to be an idealist. He said he wanted to liberate the oppressed peasantry and create the utopian state of goodwill to all by adopting anarchy. Baloney! He stole, plundered, burned, murdered and enjoyed his women to his heart's content.

In Karpowka, where my father was born, four boys in their early twenties were butchered and around the same time his uncle Dave was shot "almost for the fun of it."

"For a while," he continued, "there was in Chortitza near a sidewalk on the street—I had to pass by there, too—the body of a man with his brains literally blown out and scattered on the ground."

But Makhno's Army was not the only force my father feared. In 1918 the Bolsheviks decreed that anyone suspected of counter-revolutionary activity could be imprisoned or executed without trial. This edict was very much on his mind when one day he was detained by a group of Red Army soldiers who accused him of being a White Army spy.

Along I went to the headquarters of the secret police . . . they ransacked my suitcase . . . then I had to strip and show them my God's handiwork . . . It's kind of a nasty feeling to be exposed thus, but fortunately I had been permitted to retain my drawers . . . Right there and then I was not sure of the outcome . . . People were shot like flies every day. I was aware of it . . . The stories you read that in a moment of facing death your whole life flashes before your mind's eye are rubbish . . . You simply cease to function mentally. All of a sudden deadly silence crashed the room. One of the inquisitors had discovered my pocket notebook. He . . . started to peruse it, page by page . . . At last—finished! You may go!

Never before, never since, has a note of dismissal

sounded as blissful as that one! I was free! Free! Alive! Saved! And what was the magic of that notebook? It contained two things that disproved their theory of my being a spy. It was my diary . . . containing all the important events of the school year. Secondly it contained numerous quotations (in Russian) from the classics, notably Turgenev, Dostoevski and Tolstoy . . .

Chaos continued to reign over Russia, which was also engaged in a war with Poland that lasted from 1919 until the Treaty of Riga was signed in March 1921. By this time the fertile farms of the Ukraine, already crippled by the confiscation and destruction of crops by invading and departing armies, were experiencing a severe drought, creating a famine that lasted for the next two years. My father's poverty became so severe that he had to leave school before he had the teaching certificate he was seeking. However, with the help of his older brother, who was a certified teacher, he did manage to get a position as an elementary school teacher and for the next six years he attempted to support himself and at times his mother and younger siblings through various teaching jobs that paid barely enough to cover his own room and board. Through it all he suffered periods of near starvation, typhoid and many more brushes with death.

One of the teaching jobs Dad secured was in the village of New York, and it was here that he met and began courting my mother, much to her family's disapproval. By this time all of my grandfather's mills had been taken over by the Communists, his bank accounts frozen and most of his possessions either stolen or sold to cover his family's living expenses. Although they were still better off than my father, they were struggling to make ends meet while trying to avoid committing any "crime" that might land them in the work camps of Siberia.

In 1926 my father was denounced as an "enemy of the people" because he refused to teach his students the Communist party line and would not give up attending church, an activity now forbidden to teachers, and he decided it was no longer safe for him to remain in Russia. To pay for the numerous approvals he needed to leave the country, he borrowed money from my grandfather, who was also making plans for his family's escape. So that they wouldn't be separated during the emigration process, my parents were hastily married in a civil ceremony. Finally, with travelling funds advanced by the CPR, they were able to leave their homeland and set sail for Canada.

They settled first in the northern Ontario town of Reesor where my father purchased a small homestead. Here, after a proper Mennonite wedding, my parents' marriage was finally consummated. Since he didn't speak English and his teaching experience was of no use to him in Canada, my father turned to cutting pulpwood for a living. But this was not the kind of life he wanted, and in the summer of 1928 he sold his homestead and he and my mother joined her family in Coaldale, Alberta, where he helped out on their farm while waiting for threshing season when workers would be needed. It was during this time that my mother went into labour and after thirty-six hours of agony, assisted only by an elderly midwife, gave birth to my sister, Else.

By working on threshing crews for the rest of the summer, my father saved enough money to attend the German English Academy in Rosthern where he was offered free tuition as well as free accommodation for himself, my mother and sister. To qualify for normal school, Dad needed to pass grades ten through twelve, but since he loved learning almost as much as teaching, he enjoyed most of his time at the Academy, and by taking extra courses, he managed to graduate in two years rather than three. Every summer he went back to the threshing crews, often labouring from dawn until dusk to earn the money he needed to support his growing family. Even with this, he was often forced to borrow money, including the $40 fee charged by the doctor who delivered my second sister, Hilde.

In the fall of 1930 he moved his small family to Saskatoon and began the first of two years at the normal school. Here life was even harder for he had to supply his own accommodation. Then shortly after their arrival there, Hilde required hospitalization, which in those days was not free, and he was faced with another doctor's bill.

Through all his years of study, the subject that gave my father the greatest difficulty was English, and when he finally obtained his teaching certificate, it was conditional on improving his ability to communicate orally in this language. Still, he was assigned to a school east of Rosthern that included a teacherage, and in the fall of 1932 he was finally back in his cherished profession. As in Russia, while he didn't always get along with the school managers, he *was* popular with the students, being strict but also fair. If anyone in his classes messed around, he'd just point his finger at the offender in dead silence in such a manner that even the most troublesome student was quelled.

By the time he began teaching, however, the Depression was on and he was able to earn little more than a subsistence wage. Anything extra, such as medical treatment, meant going deep into debt, and in the winter of 1933 his growing grudge against doctors increased when it cost him half a year's salary to cover my delivery. Fortunately, within a few years he was hired as a teacher at the German English Academy in Rosthern, but until the age of forty-two, he was forced to supplement his low income by leaving his family every summer to join whatever threshing crew would hire him.[6]

For me life in Rosthern was pretty idyllic. I was a poor boy in that small Saskatchewan town with unlimited freedom to do what boys do—barefoot. There were no parents to worry about, no supervision. We were just free to roam and the only rule was that I had to be home in time for supper. Of course, my parents must have known what I was doing, but my friends and I all came from the same background and the expectation was that we'd just behave ourselves, and we wouldn't do anything nasty to anybody. I learned this latter lesson when I was

My mother never let anyone cut my hair and it was all in long ringlets, until one day the minister came to our house and mistook me for a girl. The very next day I received my first haircut.

three years old. My mother never let anyone cut my hair and it was all curly with long ringlets. One day the minister came to our house, patted me on the head and said, "How's my little *girl* today?"

"I'm NOT a girl! I'm a boy!" I said in a bit of a sassy way.

My parents chastised me for speaking to the minister in such a belligerent manner, but the next day my dad took me to the barber. My mother was upset, but Dad said, "No, it's not fair."

The elementary school in Rosthern was a two-storey, sand-coloured brick building with great wide steps. It contained twelve classrooms that could each hold at least thirty children. As a January baby, I was almost seven when I started there, six months older than any of my friends. Like the other Mennonite children, my first language was the low German dialect that we spoke at home, in the community and at church, and it was so natural to me that I thought it very strange when my Sunday school teacher, who was also my grade one teacher, said to my friends and me, "Boys, in school you have to speak English."

Still, I managed as well as the other students and passed easily into grade two where life became much more difficult. The Second World War was on and my new teacher was an English woman whose brother was in the army. She didn't like it that the Mennonites were conscientious objectors who went to work camps instead of going to war, and she took her displeasure out on us kids. In that one year alone I received nine strappings from her for the most minimal offences. Once it happened because I poked a hole in the back cover of my scribbler with a pencil. The little girl beside me said, "Teacher! Eric poked a hole in his scribbler." The teacher was there in an instant demanding that I hold out my hand for the strap. Of course, I knew better than to tell my parents about this punishment because I'd just get spanked again at home.

Because it was wrapped in customs that didn't change from year to year, my life at home was easier for me to understand. We never had a car, so most of our family activities were conducted within walking distance of our house, an unpretentious building that my mother always kept spotlessly clean. The bedrooms were upstairs and mine was a hallway of sorts that led to my sisters' much larger room. When they left home, I moved into their room and my brother Verner, who was eight years younger than me, was given mine.

Although she was raised to be a lady, my mother had quickly adapted to her changed circumstances and became an expert at creating delicious meals on a limited budget. Most of what she cooked was a mixture of Mennonite and Ukrainian dishes. Breakfast was always porridge and tea. Coffee, being expensive, was reserved for Sundays. For lunch and dinner we would have borscht or chicken noodle soup or *veraniki* filled with cottage cheese with an exquisite filled pastry for dessert. Mennonites raised a lot of pigs and at slaughtering time my dad would buy half a pig from one of our farming friends. In the summer my mother always had a huge garden, and she grew everything, including white and red currants, strawberries, raspberries, and my favourite food of all—gooseberries. She preserved everything she could harvest including wild berries and crabapples, and in the cool basement she stored huge containers of rhubarb and crockpots filled with sauerkraut that bubbled as it fermented. Sometimes during the summer we would get a ride with people who had cars and go to the South Saskatchewan River, nine miles from Rosthern, to pick chokecherries, wild strawberries and saskatoons. In the dry climate of Saskatchewan, the saskatoon bushes are huge and in August there is a profusion of large, juicy berries.

On Sunday mornings we attended the Mennonite church, which was always packed. The younger children had a Sunday school service downstairs, but once we became teenagers, although we continued to have an adult Sunday school, we were allowed to sit in the balcony and listen to my dad's choir and the regular sermon, which was a very fundamental, solid kind of service that usually held some kind of moral lesson. After church families would get together to visit and share a meal. In the summer we would often go for a picnic with our friends to an experimental farm near Rosthern, and during the winter and spring our routines were interrupted with festive occasions. At our house, Christmas celebrations began on Christmas Eve when my dad would decorate the tree with real candles. From then right through Boxing Day we feasted and visited with friends, often gathering around the tree to sing traditional songs. Easter was almost as special as Christmas, and I remember my sisters showing me how to paint eggs, which would be hidden for me to find the next morning. There was much feasting on this day as well and my mother always made a Ukrainian bread called *paska* for dinner.

Every Monday night our family would gather around the radio to listen to *Lux Radio Theatre* where Broadway plays adapted for radio were performed by the top stars of the day. For the rest of the week the radio was silent or reserved for listening to classical music, but now and then my dad would let me listen to *The Green Hornet* or *The Shadow*. To keep from disturbing anybody, I kept the volume low and scrunched up close to the radio to listen.

With no car and seldom any funds for bus or train fare, our family outings were either local or limited to the occasional day trip to Saskatoon on the train. Our parents would give us each ten cents to spend and it could take over an hour for us to decide what we would buy. We did, however, make one journey to Rosemary, Alberta, when I was six years old. My dad's widowed mother, who had also immigrated to Canada, had married a minister and settled there. My dad's youngest brother lived with them, and the whole family was coming together for his wedding. We travelled by bus, which must have been an incredible expedition for my parents, and stayed for three days. It was my first and only meeting with my grandmother, but I don't remember her even giving me the time of day.

When I was ten years old I got rheumatic fever and was so ill that the doctor told my mother I might not survive. I remember sitting on the windowsill and looking down at myself lying in bed. My mother was holding me and crying, "Don't go! Don't go!" Behind me were angels calling as clear as could be, "Come on, Eric! Come with us!" It was a true out-of-body experience, no doubt triggered by my delirium and religious belief that angels were real. After I recovered, I found out that one of my best friends, a girl in grade four, had died from the same illness. It was my first lesson in how easily friends can disappear from our lives.

Our lack of money didn't keep me or my friends from discovering the mysteries of the world around us or from creating our own fun, although sometimes we had to circumvent the rules laid down by our parents. For example, Mennonite children were not allowed comic books. However, among my circle of friends was an English boy who was happy to share his collection of comics and I spent many an afternoon at his house lost in the adventures of Captain Marvel, Superman and other superheroes.

Most of my childhood friends, however, were Mennonite farm boys and it was with them that I learned to swim in a farmer's dugout. One end of this bare-bum pool contained about ten feet of water, while the other end was shallow enough for cattle to walk in and drink. Our method of learning was to jump into the deep part and flail our way to the shallow end. Then, emboldened by this newly acquired ability, my friend Albert Rempel and I launched a home-made raft on Ross Creek, which skirted our town, and to increase the depth of our waterway, we dammed the culvert that ran under the road. The next morning there was a great hubbub in town because the creek had overflowed, flooding and damaging the road. While the town fathers and police constable could not understand how the culvert had become blocked, Albert and I were petrified with fear, but we never confessed our crime and eventually the matter was dropped.

I was always fascinated by birds, and once in a while my friends and I would steal baby owls from their nests and raise them in the hayloft of my friend's barn. They would become tame enough that we could hold them in our hands and feed them. In the fall we'd let them go. Over the years I also built up a collection of eggs from every kind of wild bird that made its home around Rostern. To preserve the eggs, I would make two pin-sized holes to blow out the insides, and then store them in a special box in my room. Years later, after I had left home, my mother found my collection and not understanding its significance, threw the eggs away.

To make a few pennies during the summer, my friends and

I was always fascinated by birds, and for my friends and me, capturing owlets from their nests and raising them ourselves in the hayloft was a great adventure. I'm the kid on the right.

I would kill gophers, a cruel practice that involved flooding the gophers' burrows, forcing them to come to the surface where we would be waiting to kill them with sticks that each had a sharp nail protruding from one end. There was a huge plague of these rodents in Rosthern so the village fathers gave us two cents for every tail we brought in. But some of the farmers would give us an additional penny if we hunted on their land, and being somewhat financially savvy, we'd always go to those places first, often collecting up to twenty-five tails in a day.

We spent much of the money we earned on hockey gear because, as with most Canadian kids in those days, hockey was our favourite sport. In fact, it was so popular that our school day was extended until five p.m. in order that the team could practise from twelve until two. Often our coaches played other roles in our lives, and for a few years the coach's position at our school was filled by our principal. During one game while executing a defensive manoeuvre, I was boarded by another player right in front of our own player's box. Not realizing that the coach was within earshot, I picked myself up and snarled, "You bugger!" Before I had a chance to skate away, my coach pulled me out of the game.

"Do you know what that word means?" he demanded, and when I shook my head, he sent me to the dressing room with instructions to go home, look the word up in the dictionary and never use it again.

At another time our coach was the town constable. We were around twelve years old by then, and five or six of us had taken to smoking in an abandoned shed behind the local hotel. One boy would steal the cigarettes from his dad's store and we'd all sit there puffing away so the whole place just steamed with smoke. I remember going home after one of these episodes and smelling cigarette smoke. Afraid of being discovered, I kept covering my mouth with my hand, certain that the smell was coming from my breath. It wasn't until much later that I realized it was actually my fingers that were stinking. One day we created so much smoke in the shed that it seeped out through some cracks. Somebody walking by noticed this and the next thing we knew the door crashed open and in marched the constable.

"Well, boys," he said, "this is the last time you smoke. Because if I ever catch you smoking again, you can't play hockey. And," he added, "I'll tell your parents."

We all quit.

I used to say that I had spent my childhood seeing my dad from the back as he was always conducting a choir. Although it was meant as a joke, it was very close to the truth for Dad's passion for music was rivalled only by his love of teaching. In his memoir he described how as a child he would beg his mother, who had a magnificent voice, to sing *Wiedersehn* or *In den Himmel ists wunderschon* when she tucked him into bed.

"She willingly complied," he wrote, "for she liked them herself, especially after her husband died a month or two later . . . Even through the darkest moments of my life these two songs have pierced the gloom as beams of hope scattering darkness and restoring the balance, and singing (and music) has forever been the sun of my life.[7]

While he described his own voice as "my croaking bass," he did have absolute pitch. He knew exactly what you were supposed to sound like and he could blow on his little instrument and tell you precisely where you should be. As a teacher in Russia he had taught numerous choirs, which, because there was often no musical accompaniment, sang a capella in four-part harmony. When he came to Canada he started a similar choir in Reesor and another for his fellow students at normal school.

During World War II when the Mennonite churches in Canada were cut off from their counterparts in Germany, my father and two other Mennonites, J.G. Rempel and D. Epp, formed an editorial committee to compile a book of German hymns. The hymnary was published eight years later and sold in Canada, the US, Germany and South America. Even before this project was finished, however, Dad had started his own book of seventy-five songs called the *Liederalbum*. The four hundred copies he self-published were all sold within three weeks, providing him with the funds for another edition. This and *Liederalbum Volume II* were both published in November 1945 and were so successful that in 1957 a BC publisher took over the printing and marketing, combining both volumes into one.[8]

In Rosthern my dad led the church choir, the men's choir, and at school the Mendelson Choir, which was composed of forty students, ten in each section. Occasionally he accepted invitations to be the guest conductor in other towns, and one Christmas he sacrificed our family gathering to conduct choirs in Tofield, Didsbury, Calgary, Rosemary and Coaldale, Alberta, earning $200, which was more than a month's salary.[9]

As Dad was an exacting conductor, his choirs were always winning prizes at choir fests throughout Saskatchewan and Alberta, and every student in our school, even those of us who were crazy about hockey, would rather have been in the choir than anything else. It was the jewel in the crown of our school, partly because it was the only activity around that involved a lot of travelling. On Sundays our house would be filled with Dad's music students. He would talk about Beethoven and Mozart, give lessons in music history and demonstrate his points by playing classical records. I remember over the years a lot of kids telling me that this was their first exposure to classical music and how grateful they were for those music appreciation days.

Much to both my own and my father's disappointment, however, I was never able to participate in his choirs, although Dad never gave up hoping. Every fall before the new school term began, he would take me to the piano and try my voice. Then he'd grimace. "Oh," he'd say, "you won't be in the choir this year. You might as well play hockey again." Had I possessed the musical talents necessary to join his choirs, my childhood relationship with my father might have been much closer. While we got along well, he was always either working at school, conducting choirs or giving music lessons, and every summer until 1942 he was away working with threshing crews to augment his salary as a teacher.

Dad was also a chess master, playing chess by mail, and he often had as many as six games going at one time. He'd exchange postcards with the other players, with a penny stamp on each card, and it was my job to take these to the post office every day. When he received a card, he would set up the game he was playing with that person, make his move, write on the card, using initials for the chessmen and numbers for the squares, and send it. During the war these unusual encryptions caught someone's attention and prompted the Mounties to check him out as a possible spy! In addition to the games by mail, Dad had two chess partners who came to the house. Sometimes I played with him, but he would never let me win.

All through my childhood my mother spoiled me with food and attention, reading to me, putting me to bed, nursing me when I was sick. But my dad had no money to spoil me with, and not being athletically inclined, he wasn't interested in the sports I played. And I wasn't good at either music or chess, which aside from teaching were his life. However, I do know he was proud of me, even though it wasn't his style to lavish praise on anyone.

My mother's spoiling didn't mean I got off without doing chores. It was my job to keep the wood box full, and every Saturday during the winter I had to fill the cistern with snow. This was a large cement enclosure, roughly eight feet wide and six feet deep, that was built into the basement. From here water was hand-pumped into the kitchen through a covered opening near the stove. My job was to carry in huge tubs of snow and dump it into this opening to keep the cistern's water level topped up.

Winter was the only time we had an indoor toilet and it

was located in my bedroom. So if anyone wanted to use the "honey bucket" as it was called, they had to do so in my room. When full, it was my job to empty this container, and I used to hang on to the pot for dear life as I carried it down our steep stairway, through the house and outside to the outhouse. Needless to say, I resented my sisters every time they came into my room to do their business.

One day when I was twelve years old I developed an agonizing toothache and needed to have the tooth extracted. Since there was no dentist in Rosthern, and we had enough money for only one fare, it was necessary for me to travel to Saskatoon by myself. It was my first trip alone to the city and one I might have enjoyed much more if I hadn't been in so much pain. Fortunately, the medical dental building was right next to the railroad station, and as soon as my tooth was pulled, I was able to catch another train back to Rosthern.

In grade seven I started working as a delivery boy for the local butcher shop. My boss was a hard-drinking kind of guy with a big red nose but an even bigger heart. He knew how poor my family was and at the end of every week he would give me the leftover hamburger to feed to my owl, never letting on that he knew darned well I was giving it to my mother. Every Saturday morning in a little shed behind his shop he would make a fresh batch of delicious, garlic-free ring baloney, and

Growing up in the town of Rosthern, Saskatchewan, I had an idyllic life in a small town. I attended a Mennonite high school where we spent most of our free time playing hockey.

eventually I was placed in charge of the cooking process. As soon as the baloney was ready, about three or four in the afternoon, some of the local drifters would appear with a case of beer, and the butcher would say, "Eric, let them have some sausage." He would allow them to stay there all night, drinking beer and eating baloney, but because there was a lot of expensive equipment inside, the shed had to be padlocked. So these men would pay me fifty cents to come the next morning on my way to church and let them out. In later years I was horrified to think of what the consequences would have been had a fire ever started while they were locked inside.

When I was fifteen, I hitchhiked to Coaldale, Alberta, where I had a summer job on the farm of my mother's brother. He had been born just before the family immigrated to Canada and was now a successful farmer, growing row crops such as beets, peas and corn as well as a variety of grains. His fields were irrigated with water from the St. Mary River that was carried to the farm through a series of small canals that criss-crossed the fields. To seal off a canal, a sheet of canvas was attached to a long stick that stretched from one side of the ditch to the other. Dirt was then shovelled onto the leading edge of the canvas to hold it in place so that it formed a small dam. All day long I would manage the water flow by resetting these dams, then just before dark I would make my last setting to water a field of wheat or alfalfa overnight. After a quick supper I'd head out to my sleeping quarters in the grainery and fall sound asleep until four the next morning when my uncle would throw a rock against the building and shout, "Eric! Time to get up!" I would head immediately out to the drenched field and make a new setting. Only then would I go into the main house for breakfast.

One of the perks of this job was that I was allowed to drive the beet truck to deliver the harvest to the beet dump. In those days it was possible for younger drivers to get a special off-highway licence so they could operate farm vehicles. My uncle's rule was that I could go to the dump and back and nowhere else, but it so happened that I was in love that summer. One day, being anxious to receive a letter from my girlfriend in Rosthern, I decided to extend my territory to the nearby town so I could stop at the post office. The main street of this little town was also the highway, and being a novice driver, I angle-parked with the back of the truck sticking out onto the road. The letter I received was much on my mind when I came out and hopped into the truck, so when I backed out, I didn't look carefully to see if anyone was behind me. Suddenly I felt a small bump. I knew at once that I must have hit somebody, but since I was going dead slow, I was sure there was no serious damage and I drove off, pretending I hadn't noticed. As I drove down the country road, I could see in my rear view mirror that the car I hit was coming right behind me, and a police car was following close behind it, but I didn't stop until I got to my uncle's farm. Fighting back tears, I jumped out of the truck and turned to face my double escort. My uncle, who had been watching this parade slowly moving down his long driveway, walked over to the guy in the car and a moment later he and the police officer were grinning. When I heard this big belly laugh from my uncle, I fled into the house, completely humiliated and certain that I was going to jail. As it turned out, my uncle paid for the damages and I was not charged for my felony. I did, however, learn a lesson.

My decision to become a doctor was triggered by a hockey accident when I was eighteen. We were playing an evening game, and during a tumble another player's skate blade slashed my leg just above the leather of my own skate. The gash required six stitches, and as the doctor was working on it, I couldn't stop watching him. Finally he asked, "You find this interesting?" When I confirmed that I did, he invited me to attend the St. John's first aid course that he taught. I did and completed it, passing at the top of the class, and this prompted him to suggest that I seriously consider becoming a doctor. Until then I had taken it for granted that I would become a teacher, and my father was pretty disappointed when I took the doctor's advice and decided to study medicine instead.

By this time I was already in grade twelve and making plans for university. One day while I was working at the butcher shop, my boss asked me what I was going to do for money. When I told him I had to borrow the funds I needed, he immediately offered to lend me the money. I was touched by his generosity but in the end elected to take the interest-free student loans offered by the university.

Our family's life in Rosthern ended in the fall of 1951. For the previous two years my dad had spent every spare moment taking correspondence courses and summer classes towards his Bachelor of Education degree, which had become a requirement for high school teachers. Now, after sixteen years of teaching, he took a year's sabbatical, sold our house and with a $1,000 grant entered his final year at the University of Saskatchewan in Saskatoon where I had enrolled as a first-year premed student.

The only accommodation our family could afford in the city was a small duplex with a paper-thin partition between the two units. The people on the other side were constantly loud, and when their music wasn't blaring us out of the house, they were fighting like cats and dogs. While Verner, who was in grade five, didn't seem to mind it, the noise was so intrusive that my dad and I did a lot of our studying in the evening at the university. But this year must have been especially difficult for my mother as she had never become fluent enough in English to communicate well with anyone beyond our Mennonite community.

Although I continued to be active in hockey and did participate in some of the university activities, my main focus was on my studies. My dad, on the other hand, lived the life of the freshman to the hilt, wearing the cap and doing the silly things freshmen often do. Consequently, he was soon very familiar with the behaviour of some of his female classmates. Coming home from classes one day I found him seated at the kitchen table. He seemed most uncomfortable and after clearing his throat, said hesitantly, "You know, Eric, there are some *loose* women on the campus."

I nodded. "Yes, I know, Dad."

His relief was expressed in an audible sigh and he said swiftly, "Oh, good, good. You know about that!"

Having earned his Bachelor of Education, my father secured a teaching position at a high school in Picture Butte, Alberta. While he and my mother and brother prepared to move to that province, I applied for a summer job at Hay River in the Northwest Territories with the Fisheries Research Board of Canada. When I went to the dean for a letter of reference, he asked me why I was choosing to work for the Fisheries Department instead of taking a medical job, as most premed students did. I told him, "Well, I'm going to be spending the rest of my life in the hospital milieu. I want to take the opportunity now to just go out into nature." He liked my answer.

Hay River is a small settlement on the south shore of Great Slave Lake. As it was linked year-round to southern Canada by the Mackenzie Highway, the town had become the main staging area for ships and barges travelling down the Mackenzie River to the Beaufort Sea, and was the centre of the commercial fishery for trout and white fish on Great Slave Lake, which is four hundred and eighty kilometres long and in some points a hundred and nine kilometres wide.[10]

Our research crew arrived at the lake in early June and stayed in a small cabin while we painted the boats and got our equipment ready. By the time the ice went out around the end of the month we were into summer weather and the days on the lake were long and pleasant with only the occasional storm. There were enough mosquitoes around to warrant mosquito netting in our tent, but I don't remember them being a problem.

My job, when the ice was gone, was to take random weights of the fish that were caught and to do a creel census. For this I was based at a fish camp next to a large plant where the fish were packed in ice before being barged to Hay River. There they were loaded onto trucks and freighted to Philadelphia, Chicago and New York. If the fish arrived within twelve days of leaving the water, they were still considered fresh by the eastern wholesalers, and most truckers made the journey in less than nine days.

As the fishermen came in, I would interview them, asking where they had fished, how long their nets were in the water and how many fish they had pulled from each net. However, most of them had more nets than they were allowed, and at first they would lie about their catch numbers. I kept reassuring them that I was working for Fisheries Research and not for the Inspections Branch, and eventually they came to trust me with the truth. It also helped that the Fisheries inspector never asked me for that information.

The man in charge of the research crew was Ross Wheaton,

Summers spent taking random weights and analyzing the catch from fishery research vessels were the beginning of a lifelong enjoyment of fishing.

a marine biologist who was only four years older than me and also attending university, and we soon became great friends. Eventually he switched from marine biology to medicine, and we went through medical school together. Throughout the summer Ross would take undergrad students out on the lake for ten days at a time to analyze the fish, and I'd get to go along when I needed a break. For this job we used a twenty-six-foot cabin boat and we would catch our own fish in nets. After taking as many as twenty-one measurements of each fish, we were left with the carcasses, far more than we could possibly eat. Sometimes a Native family would come by in their canoes and we'd give them as many as they could take, but most of the time we had to throw the fish away. So what we often did was to create gourmet meals from the livers or cheeks.

In the fall I returned to university, this time sharing a basement room with a friend. It wasn't much in terms of furnishings—a single room with two narrow beds, two desks and a hotplate—but it was ruled over by a tiny, sixty-five-year-old widow we called Mom Henry. She had already raised her own two children and she truly became a mother to us.

Normally premed takes three years to complete, but in late August of the following summer when I was working at Hay River again, checking catches at the fish camp, I received a telegram from the dean of the university offering me a spot in the medical program that fall. Apparently two people had dropped out of the program at the last minute, and the dean had been going down the list of premed students to fill the position. Because I was in camp that day and not out on the boat, I was able to reply immediately. My friend Ralph Pendleton had received a similar offer, and within two weeks we both found ourselves in medical school, each of us grateful that the cost of our schooling had just been reduced by a year.

For our first two years at medical school we studied chemistry and biology and attended labs and lectures at the university medical building. Ralph and I were among the youngest students in our class, the others being from one to three years older and, to our minds at least, much smarter. Still, we managed to hold our own and were soon part of a group that were considered the movers and shakers of the school. We organized dances and medical shows and played on the medical society's hockey team.

The rest of the time we worked and studied hard, and all of us, even the brightest students, lived in constant fear of failing. For me that fear was compounded as we studied one disease after another. Already aware that my earlier bout with rheumatic fever could result in a number of complications in later life, including a heart murmur, I soon found myself identifying with every new symptom I learned about, convinced that it was my rheumatic fever sequela kicking in. Only much later in my training did I discover that a lot of medical students wrestle with similar fears.

It wasn't until our third year in medical school that we were actually allowed to work with patients. At this time the friend with whom I had shared Mom Henry's basement suite got married, and rather than look for a new roommate, I accepted an offer that the Saskatoon City Hospital was extending to externs, as we were called, of room and board in their intern quarters in exchange for doing preoperative histories and physicals four nights a week. A common practice in those days was for surgeons to admit patients with only a diagnosis, for example, of gallstones. The patients who were scheduled for surgery on Monday morning would come in on Sunday, but there would be no accompanying history or physical. Neither the surgeon nor the patient's general practitioner had sent in any information. So right after supper we externs would scurry around, interview these people, complete a physical exam and then write out a history and physical. It was tiring but also rewarding because we got to hang out with the interns.

It was in this way that I developed my passion for surgery,

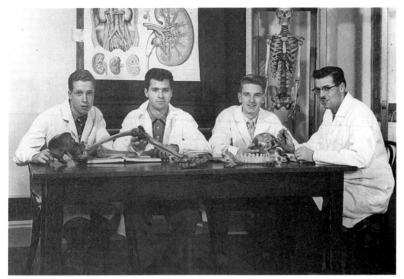

Friends and aspiring physicians work on a cadaver (I am third from left). We worked and studied hard, but all of us, even the brightest students, lived in constant fear of failing.

for even as mere medical students the externs would be called on by the surgeons to come into the operating room and help out. Thus I was able to do a lot of surgery in the evenings and on weekends. Since my entertainment allowance was limited to five bucks a month, and I wasn't smart enough to have rich girlfriends, I didn't feel I was missing out on anything by putting in these extra hours.

In early June 1956 I arrived in Hay River for my final year with the Fisheries Department. One afternoon as we were working on our gear, a Fisheries officer brought a young woman into the yard and after introducing her as Bonnie Johnson, told us that they were having a community "revue" in a few days and needed someone to be the back end of a horse for one of the skits. I was so intrigued by both the girl and the idea that I piped up, "You need a horse's ass? I'll do it!"

The eldest daughter of Olga and Oskar Johnson, Bonnie had been born and raised in the Icelandic community of Siglunes near Lake Manitoba where her parents had a large farm. When she was fourteen, she had boarded with an Icelandic family in Winnipeg so she could attend high school.

For several years in the early 1950s, Lake Manitoba's water level had reached record levels, flooding many of the farm fields so that no crops could be grown. No government aid was available for the farmers in those days, and unable to make a living under such conditions, in 1955 the Johnsons sold their cattle and moved with the youngest of their four daughters to Hay River where a year later Oskar got a job as a Fisheries inspector. While their two middle daughters continued with their schooling in Winnipeg, Bonnie was busy teaching at a one-room school in rural Manitoba. In those days it was so hard to get teachers for small rural schools that grade eleven students were able to take a six-week summer course and then teach for a year, and since Bonnie had skipped a grade, she was able to take on this job at the age of sixteen. Her class of grades one to eight included two big, shy farm boys who were nearly as old as she was.

In July the three oldest Johnson sisters travelled with their aunt and grandfather to Hay River where the younger girls were to stay with their parents. Bonnie had planned to return to Winnipeg to complete her schooling, but after she developed a crush on a Mountie, she decided, with her parents' permission, to remain in Hay River and take her final year of high school by correspondence. When I met her, she was dating the Mountie but had registered to attend summer classes in Winnipeg to obtain her graduation certificate. She would be leaving two weeks after the play was presented.

There was only time for one rehearsal before the performance, but I did my best and the skit was a hit. While Bonnie said later that she liked my legs, I had decided that I wanted her to be a part of my life. When she turned down my invitation for a date, I dictated a glowing letter of recommendation about myself, which my boss wrote on official Fisheries Research stationery and delivered to her. A few days later she consented to go for a boat ride with me. Promising her dad that I would have his daughter home by ten o'clock, I took her down to the river where the Fisheries boat was moored. It was June 21, the longest day of the year, and the sky was clear as we headed down the Hay River and onto Great Slave Lake. As we explored the shoreline, we became so absorbed in learning about each other that I didn't realize how late it was getting until my engine ran out of gas. Glancing at my watch I saw that it was just after nine.

"We've got to head back," I said as I grabbed the jerry can of fuel I had brought along and quickly filled up the tank

I fell in love with Bonnie when she was still a teenager. In those days it was so hard to get teachers for small rural schools that Bonnie was able to take on a one-room schoolhouse at the age of sixteen.

then tried to start the engine. Nothing happened. After several more failed attempts, I discovered that my fellow researchers had played a joke on me, substituting kerosene for gasoline! For some reason, Bonnie believed my explanation and between the two of us, we rowed through the night, arriving back at Hay River around four in the morning. I walked her home, but as we reached the gate, I could see her dad standing behind the glass of the front door and—panicked by images of enraged Vikings—I ran.

Fortunately, I was able to see her again for I had already made up my mind that she was the one for me, and by the time she left Hay River, we had agreed to keep in touch.

In my final year at medical school I lucked out once again. Prior to 1956, all Saskatchewan medical students had been required to take their final years of instruction at a major medical school outside of the province. But in May 1955 the Royal University Hospital had opened in Saskatoon and the following year the Saskatchewan College of Medicine was officially accepted as a teaching and research centre. Thus, our class of '57 became the first to take their entire medical course in Saskatchewan. Consequently our graduation was conducted with great fanfare with then Premier Tommy Douglas attending as our guest speaker.

I had invited Bonnie to the ceremony, but because she was busy writing her first-year exams at Ryerson University in Toronto, she wasn't able to come until the following morning. Mom Henry let her use one of the guest rooms and I was able to show her around the medical school and introduce her to my friends. The next day we took a bus to visit my parents in Coaldale, Alberta. This was her first meeting with my family and her introduction to Mennonite traditions, and because my parents always put manners before custom, she was blissfully unaware that the shorts she wore one day were not acceptable attire in Mennonite homes. As we visited the many relatives who lived near Picture Butte and in Coaldale, I tried to convince Bonnie to abandon the summer job she had taken at the CPR's Banff Springs Hotel and come with me. Long before graduation Ralph Pendleton and I had decided that we wanted to intern in a place that was warm and sunny, and after applying to several hospitals in the southern United States, we had finally chosen the Mercy Hospital in San Diego. However, Bonnie was not yet ready to make that kind of commitment, so instead we agreed to correspond but date others. I was now twenty-four years old.

The San Diego Mercy Hospital was managed by the Sisters of Guadalupe, and Ralph and I were enrolled in their rotating internship program, spending approximately two months in each of five services: surgery, medicine, paediatrics, emergency and obstetrics. We were allowed to make some adjustment to the time spent in each service as long as we did at least two months in medicine and one month in the emergency room.

During my obstetrics rotation the chief resident in charge of the house staff was Dr. Andre Bernier, a tall, robust Swiss who became agitated very easily and was a great stickler for protocol. As soon as we entered his program, we were given a written procedural guideline, one rule being that for all deliveries that required a rotating forceps manoeuvre the intern was to call the more senior resident to take over. I was almost through my two-month rotation when I was faced with a transverse arrest problem that required this manoeuvre. Although it was the middle of the night, I called the senior resident, rousing him from a sound sleep. After mumbling that he would be right over, he promptly fell asleep again, leaving the telephone receiver off the hook. Left with no way to contact him again, I delivered the baby using the rotating forceps technique as I had been taught. Everything went well and by the next morning the news of what I had done had spread throughout the department. Furious that his orders had been disobeyed, Dr. Bernier called a meeting of the house staff, some of the attending physicians, the Catholic sisters, the head nurse and myself. Here the good doctor proceeded to berate me for disobeying the guidelines. To drive home his point, he ordered me to demonstrate the procedure on a mannequin, and even though I did it correctly, he was still very agitated.

"Vy you do that rotation?" he demanded several times over.

At this point, giving in to his exasperation with the man, Ralph Pendleton drawled, "Well, hell, Andre—he is a *rotating* intern, isn't he?"

That brought the house down and the meeting was adjourned. I don't believe Andre ever did figure out what happened.

One of their strict rules was that we had to do a pregnancy

test on every woman of child-bearing age who was to undergo a dilatation and curettage (generally known as a D and C) of her uterus. One day as I was about to initiate this procedure on a sixty-year-old lady who had already been anaesthetized, I looked at one of the student nurses and said, tongue-in-cheek, "Oh, no! I didn't do a pregnancy test on her!" Instead of laughing as I expected her to do, the young nurse ran right to Sister Alexine to report my infraction. A few moments later the sister came storming into the room, ready to do battle. Then she saw the patient and, after glancing at the chart, turned to the student nurse and said, "You little twit!"

That September I looked after a very rich man in emergency who had suffered a heart attack, and after I'd left for the day, his cardiologist told him that I had saved his life. When I came back to the hospital the next morning, I was called to this man's room.

"My doctor said you saved my life," he said.

"Well, yes . . . I guess I did," I admitted, whereupon he asked me for my birth date. When I told him it was in January, he said, "On that day you'll have cause to remember me."

Later, I asked his cardiologist what that meant.

"He is one of the richest men in San Diego," he said. "It could mean anything."

Unfortunately, the following week the man died and I was sure that his prophecy died with him. Still, when January rolled around, I was half-expecting something to happen. It didn't, but the man was right—I did have cause to remember him.

I received other promises from grateful patients, most of them forgotten as soon as they returned to their regular lives. Occasionally, however, a promise was kept or at least an attempt was made to keep it. This happened with a wealthy restaurant owner from Tijuana, Mexico, who had been shot in the guts. He survived and when he left the hospital he said, "Dr. Pat, you come to Tijuana and bring your friends and I'll treat you to dinner at my restaurant."

So with six of my friends, including a couple of nurses, I went across the border to his restaurant where he welcomed us effusively and showed us to the table. "I have to leave," he said, but he called the *maitre d'* over and ordered him to, "Look after my friends." And they did. They brought us food and drinks that we didn't even order and it was a wonderful meal, but when we finished, the *maitre d'* came over and presented me with a bill. Although I suspected that he knew perfectly well that the meal was supposed to be on the house, I didn't have the nerve to object, and because as usual I had no cash on me, I had to borrow from the nurses in order to pay the bill. It took me a long time to live that one down and it became a joke among the nurses: "Don't let Eric take you to dinner. You'll have to pay for it!"

Of course, as with any intern, I did occasionally make errors. One day I was caring for a large African American patient with a bowel obstruction. In order to compress the obstruction, I passed a Miller-Abbott tube through her nose and down into her stomach. The near end of this tube protruded from the patient's nose and was divided, one part connected to an inflation device, the other to a nasogastric suction bottle. The far end of the tube contained a mercury-filled balloon which, when inflated, would work its way through her intestines, hopefully relieving the obstruction, a process that could take many hours to occur. The following day as I did my rounds, the nurse pointed out that although my patient was having bowel sounds, she wasn't passing any urine. When I asked the patient about this, she said, "Oh, I pees all right, but there's a whistling sound in the bedpan when I does!"

Curious, I examined her and discovered the Miller-Abbott tube protruding from her anus into the bedpan, efficiently sucking the urine up through the tube and into the nasogastric suction bottle! Now I was faced with two choices—either deflate the balloon and pull it all the way up and out through the patient's nose, or cut the balloon off and then pull it out.

I chose to cut the tube, but I was sharply reprimanded by the Sisters of Mercy for doing so because I had wasted a $2 tube.

The sisters were concerned with more than expenses at that hospital, and one of my run-ins with them had the potential for much more drastic consequences. Four of us interns were living upstairs in the intern quarters while a chief medical resident, a man named Jabron, lived down in the basement. Jabron, who was from Baghdad and had been through some very tough times, was a serious man who valued his sleep. At two o'clock one morning the four of us came in together, making quite a racket, talking loudly and stomping around, unaware that downstairs Jabron was getting more and more furious because we were keeping him awake. Later he told me, "I didn't want to come up and confront you because I am a very violent man. I know how to gouge out eyes and I didn't trust myself not to do something violent to one of you guys." Instead, he called the night sister at the hospital and said she must call the police to come and deal with the racket upstairs.

I was in bed when there was a knocking at my bedroom door. I stumbled out and stared blearily at the two highway patrolmen standing in the middle of the living room.

"We've had a complaint from the sister at the hospital about the racket you boys are creating," one of the officers said. By this time my fellow interns had also emerged from their rooms, and it was plain to see that we had all been sleeping. Looking somewhat sheepish, the patrolman turned to his partner and said, "Well, it's obvious that these are harmless young guys." A moment later they both left, and had it ended there the incident would have easily been forgotten. But while the rest of us returned to bed, Ralph sat and fumed about the incident. Finally he picked up the phone and dialed the hospital.

"I want to talk to the night sister," he said and when the sister came on, he demanded, "Did you phone the highway patrol?"

"Yes, I did," she responded.

"Well, you're a meddlesome old biddy!" he snarled then hung up.

The next morning the four of us received a phone call telling us not to go to work but to attend an emergency meeting with Mother Superior, the medical director and the heads of all the service departments. As we stood before the committee, the medical director said, "Mother Superior has half a mind to shut down the intern program over what you said to the night supervisor."

My mouth went dry. We were halfway through our program and if they shut us down, what would we do?

We listened in fearful respect as the other members of the committee each had a poke at us. By now Mother Superior was acting very benign, and when it was her turn, she gave a long lecture that began with, "I understand that boys will be boys . . . ," and ended with, "but Doctor Pendleton, you should not have called the night supervisor a meddlesome old biddy."

By now we interns had begun to relax and the other members of the committee were smiling as if the crisis had been averted. Then Ralph, who misjudged the situation completely, said, "But Sister, she *is* a meddlesome old biddy!"

Mother Superior exploded. "Out!" she screamed. "Get out! The four of you!"

As I left that room, I knew we were doomed, but for some miraculous reason—and quite possibly the two hours the education director had spent cajolling Mother Superior—the program was allowed to continue.

However, on the whole, life for the six of us interns was pretty heady. We were all single, carefree, like-minded and living in sunny southern California, and though we worked long days, the nuns seemed to enjoy our presence, and we received a fair amount of respect. And there was a school of nurses at the hospital!

And then, as on television, there were occasions when a

special rapport would develop with a patient. For me, it happened when a beautiful young woman, now Maureen McNeil, from Vancouver was admitted with a fractured pelvis. I was concerned and smitten, but at the appropriate time she advised me that she was soon to be married. After one month she left for home in a full body autographed cast. In what I thought was a fittingly romantic parting line, I told her in my best Clark Gable voice that she was going to require c-sections for all her deliveries and that she should think of me at that time. Many years later we met by chance in a café here. She was now married and a mother and she introduced me to her family. Apparently her obstetrician had scoffed when she told him what I had said. However, it turned out that she had required c-sections for all her deliveries.

Shortly after my arrival in San Diego I had decided to buy a car. My pay as an intern was only $150 a month, but because I was a doctor, I could get 100 percent financing. My car of choice was a Ford Fairlane, which had to be ordered directly from the factory, but before it arrived an event occurred that caused me to change my order. I was doing my rotation in Emergency when a twenty-year-old woman arrived on a stretcher. She had been involved in a head-on collision and a man who had been an occupant of the other vehicle was helping to wheel her in. While the woman was completely destroyed physically, he was as right as rain.

"How can this be?" I asked him.

"I was wearing a seat belt," he said.

As soon as I was off shift that day, I phoned the salesman and asked to have seat belts installed in the car I had ordered—two in the front and two in the back. When he said he didn't even know what seat belts were, I told him to research them and find out. By the time my new car arrived, Bonnie had joined me in San Diego and we were making plans for our future together.

CHAPTER **2**

Do What Doctors Do

By backtracking along the gravel road, Bonnie and I found the small street that led to the hospital parking lot. Here were a few outbuildings, a nurses' residence near the top of the hill and a small chapel. Access to the main hospital entrance was from a parking lot at the back of the building, and as we entered I could see the Emergency Room surgery located right near the door. Before I had time to check it out, however, we were greeted by a woman dressed in men's clothing. She had a military bearing, an English accent and a brusque manner that we learned later hid a heart of gold. She introduced herself as Gerry Jervis, the clinic manager.

"Dr. Swan has left," she said, "but I'll take you to his office." As she spoke, she led the way down a short corridor and into the clinic. Since it was Sunday, there was no one in the small waiting room so she showed me the two examining rooms then opened to the door to Dr. Swan's office.

"You'll be working in here," she said, but I'm afraid I paid little attention to the details of the room because I was so captivated by the view of Garden Bay from the window.

Adjoining the clinic was a pharmacy and a tiny laboratory. Near the furnace room, which contained an oil-fuelled boiler,

When we got out of the car at the end of Garden Bay road and looked back, we could see the twin-peaked, two-storey hospital with its double row of white verandahs and sparkling window panes.

was an on-call sleeping room. Here Gerry pointed to a bed next to a radiator pipe that ran up the wall. "That goes right up to the nurses' station," she said. "At night, whenever the doctor is sleeping here waiting for a delivery, the nurses just tap on that pipe and it clangs like an alarm right beside the doctor's head."

A small workshop in the back served as the morgue, while the laundry, she said, was in an outbuilding and had recently been upgraded from a wringer-style washing machine to a commercial machine and a gas dryer. In the kitchen we were introduced to Winnie Sundquist (née Phillips), a cheerful woman who, I was to learn, could cook anything that was brought to her, including the venison and fish that were often donated by local hunters and fishermen. As we started up the steps to the upper floor, I asked Gerry how patients were transported from one level to another, since there was no elevator.

"That's why we need two strong doctors," she said.

The upper storey contained the operating room, which

doubled as a delivery room. It was a very rustic facility and contained a truly Third World operating table with four iron legs. Raising, lowering and tilting, she explained, was accomplished by inserting bricks under the legs. When more than one woman was in labour, the second mother-to-be was placed on the table in the small x-ray room.

The nurses' station, recovery room and wards were also located on this floor. Most of the wards faced the water. There were two four-bedders at each end, one for males and the other for females, a private ward, and a two-bed paediatric ward that could be converted to a four-bed ward in a pinch. A two-bed maternity ward was located in the sunroom that overlooked the harbour, and there was a nursery with three bassinets. (In those days the newborns were kept in a separate room and brought to their moms for feeding.) Two communal bathrooms and a single bathtub were shared by all patients.

Gerry introduced us to Ivy Potts, the only registered nurse on duty, and her single assistant, a licensed practical nurse. Since there was no one needing medical attention, when the hospital tour was over, Bonnie and I left to find Dr. Swan's house where we were to stay until his return.

The two-bedroom cottage had been built in 1941 as a doctor's residence and had a similar design to the four other cottages that were built and managed by the Columbia Coast Mission as "Aged Folk Guest Houses." While a thickly wooded area lay at the back of the doctor's cottage, the front faced the beach and had a lawn with a few flowers planted around the edges. We both marvelled that the Swans, who had three young children, were able to cope with such a small home, but we were delighted by its close proximity to the hospital.

A few months later the value of this was brought home to me when I was called to treat the cook on a pleasure boat called the *Friendship Seven* that was moored in the bay. After tending to the patient, I was invited on deck for a beer, and during the course of our conversation the owner, who was from San

Francisco, asked where I lived. I pointed at our cottage, which was only about seventy-five yards from the hospital.

"So how long does it take you to get to work?" he asked.

"About ninety seconds," I responded.

"Wow!" he exclaimed. "My commute is ninety minutes."

Bonnie and I spent our first night settling in and taking a brief walk to familiarize ourselves with our new neighbourhood. Early the next morning I returned to the hospital, ready for duty. It was Monday morning and there were many more staff members present, but the only other practitioner was Dr. Peter Stonier, a stocky kind of guy who, I was to discover, liked to play practical jokes. Before we did the morning rounds he introduced me to the matron, Elizabeth Smith, a sturdy Scottish woman with a thick brogue, an authoritative, no-nonsense manner punctuated by a wonderful sense of humour and a lovely giggle.

There were no difficult cases that morning, and after a brief visit with each patient we went downstairs where I met the hospital administrator, a tall, rather unkempt man who always seemed to have a cigarette dangling from his mouth. He had been hired earlier in the year when the hospital was facing a financial crisis, and through dedicated service and careful management he was gradually bringing it back to solvency.[11]

His secretary, Pixie Daly, was a one-woman band, handling not only the secretarial duties, but also admitting patients and even taking x-rays and doing lab work when no one else was available. Pixie was married to John Daly who later became famous in *Fishing With John*, a book written by his second wife, Edith Iglauer.

With rounds and introductions over, I went into my office to hold my first clinic. Although I was understandably nervous, with my grounding at the medical school in Saskatchewan, and my year of surgery in San Diego, I was sure I could handle anything that came along. But I must admit I wasn't quite prepared for Beaula, an immense sixty-five-year-old woman with five men's names tattooed on her thigh. She seemed to take an immediate liking to me, and as I examined her, she explained that the tattoos were the names of her five deceased husbands. I was slightly alarmed when she said she thought that "Eric" would look good tattooed among the others.

My next patient came in with his twelve-year-old nephew. Charlie Klein was a tough logger with a deep cut on his forehead. Pleased at this even minor chance to use my surgical skills, I prepared to freeze the area before suturing the laceration, but as I attempted to apply the local anaesthetic, the man stopped me.

"No, doc," he said, "no freezing for me. I want Michael to see how a real man handles a thing like this."

Since the patient's decision is final, I put the anaesthetic away and got on with the job, and while it hurt me to do it this way, the man never made a sound.

Late that afternoon Gerry Jervis came into my office.

"You need to make a house call to see Marian Bilcik's new baby," she said, obviously unaware that I'd never made a house call in my life.

"What do I do?" I asked, collecting my bag.

Somewhat impatiently she replied, "Well, do what doctors do!"

Pete Stonier was slightly more helpful. "Just wing it," he suggested. "Pretend you know what you're doing."

The house was a nice-looking bungalow about three miles from the hospital. Marian greeted me at the door, and as she led me to the baby's room, we were watched carefully by four petite girls who were as alike as peas in a pod.

A shy, soft-spoken woman, Marian sensed my unease and guided me through the process of examining the baby, and as soon as I focussed on the infant's symptoms, my own training took over. Infant respiratory problems in the late sixties were worrisome because you never knew when a simple cold would turn into pneumonia, which was often fatal. Most doctors took no chances and prescribed penicillin for even the mildest respiratory infections. As I examined this baby, however, I was sure there was no pneumonia.

"Call me if she doesn't get better," I said as Marian saw me off.

Years later we shared a laugh, remembering how young and nervous I had been on that visit.

As the days passed, I gradually developed more confidence, but I still faced some unexpected medical challenges. One weekend afternoon when I was the only doctor present, a man came into the clinic with a bad tooth that he wanted pulled.

"You need a dentist," I told him.

"There isn't one," he said.

I shook my head. "But I've never pulled a tooth before."

"Well," he said, "you better get a book and learn. The doctors here pull teeth." Then he settled himself in a chair. "I'll wait."

So I found a book on regional anaesthesia and after studying what I had to do, I injected the anaesthetic into his lower jaw. This location made the freezing trickier, and I wasn't even sure it took or if he was just being tough, because my patient just lay there without making a sound while I extracted the tooth.

A few days later I had to deal with another extraction—this one on a great big, mean-looking German shepherd. The dog had a toothache and the owner, Albert Martin, wanted me to pull the tooth. Since there was no vet in the area, and the animal appeared to be completely obedient, I agreed, and while Albert held him, I froze the area and extracted the tooth. That evening after taking a short walk, Bonnie and I stopped at the local pub and each ordered a drink, not realizing that we looked more like teenagers than a twenty-one- and a twenty-six-year-old adult. Mistaking us for kids from the Malibu youth camp, the bartender asked for identification before he would bring our order. Neither of us had any.

"Then I can't serve you," he said.

However, there was something familiar about the man, and suddenly I recognized him as the owner of the German shepherd. As he started to turn away, I asked, "How's your dog doing?"

Surprised, he looked at me closely and then grinned. "Oh! Oh, you're the doc!" he exclaimed. "What can I get for you?"

My two-week locum passed swiftly, and by the time Alan Swan returned I knew I never wanted to leave this place. Five years older than myself, Al was a quiet, reserved man who was very reluctant to draw attention to himself, and probably one of the most honest men you could ever meet. He was the son of a minister and grew up in Vancouver, though he moved to Toronto with his family during the war. While serving in the navy, he studied medicine, and for a time he was posted on the West Coast where he served as an extern at St. Joseph's Hospital in Victoria. There he met Rosa, who was an obstetrical nurse from Duncan. They married just before he graduated from Queen's University School of Medicine in 1953. After interning at St. Paul's Hospital in Vancouver, he practised briefly in Duncan before coming to the Sunshine Coast in October 1954.[12]

When I arrived at the hospital on the morning of his return, Al had already made his rounds, and after a preliminary exchange of information on the cases I'd been looking after, he said, "I understand you like it here, and people like you. Pete Stonier is leaving in June and this practice is too busy for one doctor. Why don't you stay? We could become partners."

I didn't have to think about it. "Great!" I said. There was a slight pause and then I asked, "What do we do now?"

Alan smiled. "Well, we shake hands on it," he said.

So we shook hands and became partners, and that's how we spent our entire careers together. We didn't need anything more formal.

That evening our two families got together to celebrate the

Dr. Alan Swan was quiet, reserved and one of the most honest men you could ever meet. Upon our arrival, Al and his wife Rosa took us under their wings.

new partnership and to discuss living arrangements. A few days earlier Bonnie and I had moved into a housekeeping unit at Lowe's Motel, just down the street from the cottage, but we needed something more permanent. Dinner gave us a chance to meet Alan's wife, Rosa, and their three children, four-year-old Eleanor, two-year-old Martin and eleven-month-old Trevor. Rosa, though a nurse, had given up her career to devote herself to Alan and their children.

Before we left that evening, it was decided that the Swans would move to Sechelt, while Bonnie and I would remain in Pender Harbour, taking over their house. As a growing number of Alan's patients were from the Sechelt and Gibsons areas of the coast, he had recently established a weekly one-day clinic in Sechelt, renting quarters above the Bank of Montreal on the south side of Cowrie Street. Moving his family to Sechelt would mean he could expand his practice there to six days a week and avoid the long drive from Garden Bay.

Although she would have preferred living in Vancouver, Bonnie quickly settled into her new home, busily sewing curtains by hand—since we could not afford to purchase a sewing machine—and scrounging furnishings. Soon she was also hand-sewing a layette for our baby, which was due to arrive in February.

Meanwhile, I was continuing to learn about my new practice and the effort that a Pender Harbour doctor was expected to make to provide medical aid to his patients. This was brought home to me near the end of September when our clinic received a message that there was a watchman in need of medical attention at a Deserted Bay logging camp.

"Someone's got to go up there, Eric," Al Swan said. "Do you want to go?"

"Yeah, but where is it?"

"Oh, just up Jervis Inlet," Al told me. "The water taxi will pick you up at the government dock."

It was a clear, sunny morning and I felt as if I was playing truant as I walked down the wharf to the twenty-six-foot water taxi. The boat appeared clean, its lapstrake hull looked seaworthy, and the Chrysler Crown engine seemed well cared for. At the helm was a stocky tugboat man in his mid-thirties who introduced himself as Bill Thompson.

"Should be a good trip," he said, and after showing me where to sit, he released the mooring lines and we were off.

"This is Jervis Inlet," Bill said as we zoomed past wooded islands and mainland shores that ranged from grassy beaches to high granite cliffs, some of them rising straight from the water, others darkened by pristine waterfalls catapulting over their sides. A while later he announced that we were heading northward up Prince of Wales Reach, which would lead into Princess Royal Reach. "Deserted Bay's at the north end of Princess Royal," he explained, "on the east side of the reach."

Since all of the waterways looked pretty much the same to me, I had no idea when one ended and the other began,

Red Nicholson's *White Arrow* took us on many adventures. On weekends we would also go sailing in his small sailboat *Our Turn*, keeping in sight of the hospital—if they needed me, the nurses would hang a sheet over the balcony railing.

but I was loving the trip, and by the time we reached the logging camp I was making plans to purchase a boat of my own.

A short trail led from the dock to the watchman's quarters, a dark, dingy shack with small windows and meagre furnishings that included a little wood heater and the bed on which my patient was lying. He was a swarthy man dressed in soiled logging clothes, and the expression on his unshaven face was not welcoming. Certainly he would not submit to an examination, but from my observations and the few symptoms he unwillingly described, I suspected he had suffered a stroke. When I told him so and suggested that he come with me to the hospital, he flatly refused.

"I'm staying right here," he said. "I didn't call for you. Now go away."

There was nothing I could do or say to change his mind, so

I turned around and returned to the water taxi. Four hours later I was back at the hospital.

"Well," I told Al, "it was a wonderful trip, but we didn't do very well financially. Since he didn't call us, we can't even charge him for the visit."

"That's not all," Al retorted. "We're also out $25 for the water taxi."

When I told Al and Pete Stonier that I wanted to buy a boat, they offered me the use of a small sailboat they shared with their friend Red Nicholson, called the *Our Turn*, as in, "our turn to have it." Bonnie and I spent many hours exploring with this boat, and on weekends when I was on call we would go sailing in the bay, keeping in sight of the hospital. If they needed me, the nurses would hang a sheet over the balcony railing. A green sheet meant come in the next one or two hours, while a red sheet meant come now!

One of the benefits of our practice was that we got to know many unique characters, and a favourite of mine was a lovely Sechelt elder, Mary Jackson. I was her GP for nine years and over that time she made frequent visits to my office. Occasionally she would cut off discussion about her medical concerns to ask if I could lend her ten dollars. When I obliged, she would thank me and promise to repay the loan soon. After this had happened several times, she would arrive with one of the beautiful baskets that she had made and was now offering for sale. I would ask her how much it cost and the amount was always ten dollars more than what she owed me. Over the years we built up a fine collection of Mary's baskets, even though we gave some as gifts to friends and family.

A known shoplifter, who was also a frequent visitor to my office, once presented me with the gift of a fairly hideous bow tie. Not wanting to hurt her feelings, I thanked her and thereafter kept it in my desk to put on whenever she had an appointment. A few years later I wore the tie to a costume party and

Mary Jackson was a lovely lady, a kind and gentle basket-maker who helped keep the church and school clean.

during a conversation with Morgan Thompson, the owner of our local men's clothing store, he suddenly exclaimed, "Now I know what happened to that bow tie!" Then he told me that it had gone missing from his store many years earlier, and although he had suspected my shoplifter had taken it, he had never done anything about it.

Another memorable character was Lars, an old-timer who lived near our cottage. One day he visited me at the clinic, and after examining him I said I needed a urine sample. Since he couldn't produce one right away, I suggested he go home with the specimen bottle and return it when he was able to do the job. A few hours later he knocked on the door of our cottage and when Bonnie answered he handed her a dripping wet bottle.

"Doc asked me to bring this to him," he explained.

Hastily Bonnie thrust the jar back at him and said he had

to take it to the hospital. After he left, she spent a long time scrubbing her hands.

One of our favourite characters who was also a great story-teller was Joe Gregson, a widower with no next of kin who "adopted" the Swan and Paetkau kids. He was one of the last surviving veterans of the Boer War, and one day when he was in his nineties, he announced, "When I was in the Boer War, they put saltpetre in our food to make us lose interest in women. And you know what? It's starting to work!"

Canon Alan Greene, who had been superintendent of the Columbia Coast Mission from 1936 to 1959, also had a wealth of stories, many of them about his years on the mission boats that brought church services and aid to remote coastal settle-ments. Many years later as he was sitting beside me during a service in St. Hilda's Church in Sechelt, he collapsed. My first reaction was that he had died, and since he was an old man, I thought, "What a fitting ending for this man of God." I considered leaving him be, but all around me people were say-ing, "Eric, do something!" So we laid him on the bench and I started CPR. He was revived, but I don't think he appreciated my efforts. He was ready to meet his maker.

Aside from the problems associated with the antiquated oper-ating table, surgery at the old hospital in Pender Harbour was always a challenge. Most of the time we used an open drop ether anaesthetic where the patient's face is covered with a porous mask onto which liquid ether is administered, one drop at a time. Whenever I was on my own at night doing emergency surgery, I had no choice but to start the anaesthet-ic, turn the job over to the nurse to monitor, and then with the assistance of another nurse, perform whatever surgery was required. With a dilatation and curettage of the uterus, which was a relatively simple procedure, I would administer the ether until the patient was in a deep state of anaesthesia, run around and perform the surgery, and then allow her to wake

Canon Alan Greene and MLA Isobel Dawson cut the ribbon on the Green Court retirement complex in Sechelt. THE PENINSULA TIMES AND THE ALSGARD FAMILY.

up in her own time. There were other occasions, however, when outsiders were commandeered to stand in for one job or another. Such was the case when Al and I were presented with a motor vehicle accident victim who had major internal injuries and needed immediate surgery. However, in the eyes of the patient's uninjured buddy I was obviously very young and inexperienced.

"You better know what you're doing, Doc," he warned me in a threatening voice, "or else!"

That's when Staff Sergeant Tick Payne, our local Mountie, stepped in, grabbed the man by the scruff of the neck and seat of the pants and hustled him out of the building with instructions not to come back.

It was decided that Al would give the anaesthetic and I would do the surgery, but since it was late in the evening there was no nurse to assist me. When Tick walked back into the room, we told him that as an encore he would have to be my scrub nurse. He did as he was told without fainting, and the surgery was successful.

The ignorance of some of the mothers I dealt with was another challenge. One day a baby girl that I had delivered three months earlier was brought into the hospital weighing less than her birth weight. I asked the mother what she was feeding her baby and she said she was giving it half-strength milk and some apple juice. The infant was marasmic (malnourished) in the extreme and, according to the mother, shitting all the time. Nothing was adding up until finally, suspecting it might be some type of an allergy, I asked the mother what kind of milk she was using.

"It's in a blue bottle," she said.

Now I was totally befuddled. "What is the name on that milk bottle?"

"Phillips."

"Milk of Magnesia?" I gasped.

"Yeah!"

Wow! That baby had been surviving on the apple juice! Fortunately, we did get her turned around and she grew up to be a healthy adult.

Of course, she wasn't the only child with nutritional problems. Another woman came to see me, and when her baby began to fuss, she pulled a Coke bottle out of her purse, removed the cap, stuck a nipple in its place and nourished the child that way.

On another occasion, a patient arrived in my office to say that she had terrible cramps in her legs. My examination revealed large, distended veins, and wanting to find the cause of this, I asked her to remove her jeans so I could feel her stomach. After some hesitation she did as I requested, and that's when I discovered she was about seven months pregnant with an active baby. Her belt had been cinched so tight on her jeans that the pregnancy hardly showed.

"Have you had anything peculiar happening in your stomach?" I asked.

"Oh, sure," she said in Norwegian-accented English. "I got a lot of gas in dare."

When I told her she was going to have a baby, she said in amazement, "Is dat so?"

I said, "You must have been sleeping with a man."

She denied that, but she did admit that she was working on a fish boat, and every once in a while her fishing partner got into her bed and did funny things to her. When it came time for the delivery, the partner brought her to the hospital and said that I should keep her there while he went fishing. Then he asked how much it would cost. I told him $100 and inquired what he was going to do about the baby. "You'll have to give it away, Doc, because she doesn't want to keep it. She'll toss it a bone once in a while, but otherwise she won't look after it."

The Garden Bay community came alive at Christmas time, with decorated trees everywhere and a steady round of parties, several at private homes and one at the nurses' residence. We decorated a tree of our own and on Christmas Day, since we had no family close enough to visit, we invited Frank Ball to come for dinner.

Frank, a short, good-natured little guy who could fix anything, was the maintenance worker at the hospital and the nearby Columbia Coast Mission's Aged Folks Guest Homes. He had emigrated from England at the age of twenty-one, a year before WWI, and joined the Canadian forces. Although a skilled carpenter, he spent the war years looking after infantry horses at Pincher Creek, Alberta. After he was demobilized, he worked as a cowboy until WWII when he signed on as a carpenter at Victoria's Yarrow Shipyards. In the 1950s he began crewing for Canon Greene on a Columbia Coast Mission boat. As they shared a love of chess, the two became great friends, eventually becoming so well known as the "Canon-Ball" team that someone composed a ditty to the tune of "The Wabash Cannonball," which was sung at parties and around campfires. The punch line at the end of the song was, "And Canon Green and Cannon Ball."[13]

This was Bonnie's first attempt at cooking a full Christmas dinner, and she had worked hard to make it perfect for Frank and me. At dinner time she proudly carried the golden brown turkey to the table for me to carve. Her embarrassment was acute when I cut into the breast and discovered that the bird wasn't quite cooked. Still, we managed to salvage enough meat from the edges to provide a meal and with all of the other dishes she had prepared, we left the table feeling well and truly stuffed.

Jackie and Pete Stonier were among the friends that we made in Garden Bay. They had one child and Jackie was pregnant with their second. One night near the end of her pregnancy, they came over for dinner and as the four of us were playing cards, Pete said, "Eric, one of these nights I'm going to phone you in the middle of the night and tell you Jackie's in labour and get you to scurry over to the hospital, only it won't be true." I didn't bother to ask him why he would do such a thing because by then I was growing used to his penchant for practical jokes. His call came at two o'clock the next morning.

"Eric! Jackie's in labour. This is no joke!"

"Of course it isn't, Pete," I said and hung up. Certain that it *was* a joke, there was no way I was going to move from my bed.

"But what if it's not a joke?" Bonnie worried. "You have to go, Eric. If it's a practical joke, that's what it is."

So I went, entering the hospital at the same time that Jackie came in through the other door. The nurse helped her onto the stretcher, but before she even had time to undress, the baby arrived. I just managed to catch it.

Later, looking very shamefaced, Pete said, "That was not a good thing to have done to you, Eric."

Unlike the snow-covered prairies, and sunny San Diego, our first winter on the coast was grey and rainy. Absorbed as I was with my medical duties, I scarcely noticed the weather, but Bonnie was finding it hard to cope with the dreary dampness. Although we had been welcomed into the Garden Bay community and people were kind to both of us, she was so much younger than any of our new friends that she felt like a misfit and was often very lonely. So when one of my patients offered us a dog, we were quick to accept, thinking it would make a perfect companion for her. Mingi was already fully grown and a mongrel in every sense of the word, but he loved Bonnie without reserve and soon refused to be separated from her.

Meanwhile, Al Swan and I developed a schedule where we each worked five days on and two days off. During his off-time Bonnie and I would move into the Swan's home in Sechelt so I could manage the clinic there, while the Swans stayed in our house or on their boat, the *Cygnet*, which was moored in Garden Bay. Every Sunday morning we would settle Mingi in the back seat of our car and make the long drive to Sechelt. Unfortunately, travelling on the narrow, curving road did not agree with the dog and by the time we reached Kleindale, a small settlement on the main highway, roughly ten kilometres south of Garden Bay, Mingi would have vomited all over the back seat of the car. Bonnie, who was suffering from car sickness herself, would be retching as we cleaned up the mess. After putting up with this for several trips, I began giving Mingi a shot before we left home so he couldn't vomit. Instead he now drooled. And drooled. No matter how many newspapers we placed in the back, that dog had the car totally drooled out by the time we got to Sechelt. (I had little sympathy with Bonnie's car sickness until we also moved to Sechelt and I shared the drive to Garden Bay with Al. As a passenger, I began experiencing the same nausea. Since Al suffered from the same ailment, we would switch positions halfway to our destination.)

In February 1960 Bonnie was admitted to the hospital in labour. Expecting a smooth delivery, we were dismayed to find that the baby was presenting in an awkward position. Consequently, her labour was long and hard, and through it all Mingi kept guard outside of the ward room window, whimpering and whining to be let in. So long as the head nurse was on duty, no one dared to allow a dog on the ward, but as soon as she left for the evening, the nurse in charge, Joe Doney, opened the door and said, "Okay, Mingi, come on in. You might as well lie under the bed."

After a day and a night the baby was still not budging, and since it was too stormy to transport Bonnie to Vancouver, we had an obstetrician fly in to Garden Bay to perform a Caesarean section. Baby Karin did not breathe for several minutes and for some time after her birth we were concerned that she might have suffered brain damage. Al told us later that he had watched her carefully for those few months and breathed a big sigh of relief when it was obvious that our daughter was fine.

In the spring of 1960, as Pete Stonier arranged to leave for Cleveland where he planned to study obstetrics, Al and I started looking for someone to replace him. But first we had to deal with an unexpected disaster.

CHAPTER 3

A Doctor for All Reasons

Gerry Jervis was an efficient bookkeeper and a formidable receptionist. She had been an officer in the army during the war and she ran such a tight ship, telling us what we could spend money on and what funds were coming in, that both Al Swan and I figured we were doing fine financially. Since I had a year of surgery under my belt, we were able to do operations that had previously been sent to Vancouver, and when the community discovered this, our practice had become busier and busier. So when Gerry announced one day that we were broke and would have to borrow money from the bank to pay our expenses, we were stunned.

"No way," I said. "I've been so busy!"

"Yes," she agreed, "but no one is paying for your services."

So the three of us sat down and went over the accounts, item by item.

The spending was easy to identify and included rent for the clinics, telephone and utility fees, transportation costs, staff expenses and medical supplies. The income was a little harder to track down since much of our practice was made up of welfare recipients and seasonal workers who weren't always able to pay their bills. Some fees were paid by government agencies such as the Department of Health and Welfare, the Department of Indian Affairs, and the Worker's Compensation Board, but the amounts they set for specific treatments were often far lower than our expenses. Our customary fee for a woman's confinement, for example, was $100, but this covered all of the prenatal care, the delivery and a six-week postpartum examination. On top of that, we were handing out $20 worth of vitamins to each of these patients for free. The Department of Indian Affairs limited the fee for a Native woman's confinement to $25. In the same way, we would charge a patient who had suffered a heart attack $80 for treatment, barely covering our expenses, but the Welfare Department would only pay 42 percent of that amount. Many of our patients who were not covered by any government agency had private insurance coverage, such as United Home Security, but this company would send their payment for our services to the patient with the suggestion that they endorse the cheque and give it to their doctor. Needless to say, several down payments on TV sets were made with cheques that were obviously meant for us. Our best source of income was from the Medical Services Association (MSA), a medical insurance plan paid for by employers and used by most of the logging companies. This service paid the exact amount we billed.

One of our major expenses was for the water taxis that took us to the logging camps up the inlets. Gradually we discovered that flying to these camps saved us both time and money, but it still cost us more for airfare than the fee that the Worker's Compensation Board would pay. Then we received an unexpected tip from Al Campbell, a veteran pilot and owner of Pacific Wings Sky Taxi (later Tyee Airways). Al was a friendly, good-looking man who had arrived on the Sunshine Coast the same year I did. He ran his airline with skill and compassion, often transporting passengers in and out of the inlet logging camps for free when they had no money to pay their fares. As a result, he was operating on a budget almost as tight as our own and sympathized with our dilemma.

"You shouldn't be paying for the aeroplane," he said one day when he was flying me home from a logging camp visit. "You should charge it to the logging company." He assured me that it wouldn't hurt his feelings to extract the airfare directly from the logging camps. Following his advice, we sent out notices to all the logging camps advising them that we would no longer be paying our own airfare.

One day when I was at Pete Jackson's logging camp, a float plane arrived with a mechanic, Bill Weinhandle, who had been called in to do some urgent repairs. He charged $50 an hour and Pete said the job was worth the expense. He wasn't impressed with our business smarts when I told him we received $40 for attending a WCB case that took three to four hours of our time.

We continued to pay for trips to private homes until one day when I responded to a medical call in Doriston, a small

Pete Jackson, a gyppo logger at Deserted Bay, always made us welcome at his camp, but we eventually discovered that flying to logging camps cost us more for airfare than the fee that the Worker's Compensation Board would pay.

settlement at the north end of Sechelt Inlet, near the entrance to the Skookumchuck Rapids. When we were flying back to Sechelt, the pilot, Fred Ritter, told me that my patient's son had paid him for the flight. "I don't know why you guys don't bill your patients for all of your flights," he said. Since I could only bill the medical plans $12 for a house call and the flight cost $40, we were always losing money on them, so it made sense to do as Fred suggested. Surprisingly, we received no complaints from our patients for doing so.

The pharmacy we were running out of our clinic was also costing us a lot of money because many patients weren't paying for the medication we handed out. Since Ben Lang was already operating two drugstores on the Sunshine Coast, one in Gibsons and another in Sechelt, we made the tough decision to stop dispensing drugs from our own office.

It was around this time that I joined the local volunteer fire brigade, and since the members assumed that a doctor could read, write and do arithmetic, I was given the post of secretary-treasurer. When we needed funds to adapt a donated barge, the *Texada Queen*, into a self-propelled unit for fighting marine fires, I joined the rest of the membership in canvassing from house to house for donations. As I was unaware which patients were not paying their bills, I didn't understand why my request for funds from one householder caused him such embarrassment. When I told him that the money was for the fire brigade, his relief was evident, and with a magnanimous gesture he handed me ten dollars. Later I discovered that he owed me $100 for a delivery, but as far as he was concerned, we were now square!

Determined to cut whatever costs we could in our practice, Al and I were excited when we saw an advertisement in a medical magazine. A Saskatchewan doctor was retiring and selling all of his equipment for $400. The list of gear included many tools we could use, so we made contact and sent him the money. We waited anxiously, and when the packing crate finally arrived, we opened it immediately. The contents were disappointing. There was nothing useful and we didn't have a clue what many of the items were, although we suspected the foot-long thermometer might have been intended for horses, and we were sure the forceps and direct blood exchange transfusion set were from World War I. The ECG machine that we had most anticipated turned out to be an old smoke drum machine, the kind of unit that hadn't been used since 1910. This, at least, we were able to use as a trade-in on a modern ECG machine. The salesman gave us a $25 allowance for it, but when we asked him how we should send the old machine to him, he said, "Don't send it. Just throw it in the ocean!"

With our finances somewhat under control, Al and I turned our attention back to finding a replacement for Pete Stonier. We listed the position with the BC College of Physicians and Surgeons, and just as Al had previously experienced, we received a lot of calls from doctors who were more interested in securing a free holiday on the Sunshine Coast than they were in joining a medical practice. Finally we decided that we would accept the first doctor who didn't phone us collect. His name was Walter Burtnick and even over the phone we could tell that he had a pretty good sense of humour.

Walter was born in Trail, BC, where he developed a love for the outdoors, particularly fishing and hunting. He worked in logging camps and house construction before he responded to his true calling as a family doctor. As soon as we met him, Al and I knew we had a winner. The same age as Al Swan, Walter was over six feet tall, and everything about him was big. He was strong and his hands were so huge that it was hard to imagine him suturing a wound or making a sensitive examination, and yet he did so with amazing gentleness and dexterity. Always comfortable to be around, he never got angry and his patients loved him. He also shared our own ideas on how a medical partnership should work, including our solution for preventing doctor burnout.

Each of us had worked during our training years with old GPs who had never kept up to date on medical changes and were unaware of new treatments that could improve the lives of their patients. To prevent this, we established a system where each partner would work for four years and then take the fifth year off for further training away from the Sunshine Coast. To make this financially feasible, we would divide our four years' income over five years so the person taking the sabbatical wouldn't starve while he was away. It was decided that since Al Swan had been practising the longest, he would take the first leave of absence as soon as we were able to get our finances in order.

Meanwhile, Walter would take over the main duties at the Garden Bay clinic, and I would assist Al in Sechelt, both of us travelling to Garden Bay for emergencies, to deliver babies, do elective surgery, attend our own patients and relieve Walter two days a week. In turn, he would come to work at the Sechelt practice when we needed to be relieved. (For his first few years in Pender Harbour, Walter put so many miles on his car that he wore out a tire a month.)

Bonnie and I rented a cottage on the waterfront within walking distance of Sechelt

Dr. Walter Burtnick, our next partner, was an ardent fisherman who even built his own boat. His hands were so big that it was hard to imagine him suturing a wound or making a sensitive examination, and yet he did so with amazing dexterity.

Village. Of course, Bonnie was delighted because she no longer had to endure the car-sick drives from Pender Harbour, the Red and White store delivered groceries right to our door, and she could now take Karin out to the shops in her stroller. Soon she had a group of younger friends that she could relate to, and even took on the job of vice-president of the newly formed Sechelt branch of the Hospital Auxiliary, so although I was still away much of the time, she was no longer lonely.

The Sechelt clinic above the Bank of Montreal had been operated by Dr. William McKee until September 1959 when he moved his practice into his own home[14] then pulled up stakes and left the district shortly after Al Swan took over the clinic. The building was accessed by a long stairway that led into a waiting room and reception/office area. Beyond this was Al's larger office with big windows that faced the street, and my office, which was about one-third the size and had a small window. A much smaller and windowless room between our offices housed the x-ray machine and a bed where we could do minor procedures such as pulling teeth or sewing up lacerations.

While we referred more serious operations to hospitals in Vancouver, we did do routine procedures at Garden Bay, and in this we were given an unexpected boost when Tom Masterson joined our team. An older man, Tom had been practising as a surgeon in Vancouver when he suffered a heart attack and was told to take it easy for the next six months. He had purchased a place in Pender Harbour and heard that we were looking for a GP. By this time Walter had already joined our partnership, but we welcomed Tom to our clinic, and since he was qualified to do major surgeries, we started doing these at Garden Bay.

The operating room, however, continued to be a challenge, especially when the help we needed wasn't immediately forthcoming. This happened when Walter and I attended a young mother who had an uneventful delivery but wouldn't stop bleeding. We finally recognized that she had torn her cervix along with the uterine artery and was bleeding out on us. The only way we could stop the bleeding was literally to hold bi-manual pressure on the uterus, a manoeuvre that meant some-one had to stand with his hand in her vagina and squeeze her uterus from above. The two of us spent the whole night taking turns at doing this while we waited for a specialist to arrive from Vancouver the next morning. In the meantime we were able to transfuse her with blood that the police brought from Sechelt, by water taxi from Powell River, and also from local donors. After about fifteen units of blood the bleeding stopped, so when the specialist finally arrived, he didn't have to do anything.

The inadequacy of the operating room was only one of many frustrations we were experiencing with the old hospital; it was simply too small, too old, and too far away for the major-ity of the Sunshine Coast's residents. As early as 1951, people in Gibsons had begun lobbying for a second hospital, prefer-ably located in their area, and by the time I arrived in 1959, the urgency of this need had increased because the population of the Sunshine Coast from Port Mellon to Egmont was now over 9,000 people.[15] In December of that year a district-wide vote had approved the formation of Hospital Improvement District No. 31 to plan for the construction of a new hospital. Along with my colleagues, I was on the building committee and we spent many hours going over plans and preparing briefs to the provincial government for funding and project approval. Of course, we knew that it wasn't going to happen overnight, and in the meantime we continued to do the best we could with what we had.

There were times, however, when we were called on to per-form procedures in settings even more challenging than those we dealt with at the old hospital, as happened the afternoon I was called to the home of a lady on the Sechelt Indian Reserve. She was already in active labour, and since there was no way she would make it to the hospital in Garden Bay, I knew I would have to do the delivery right there. The only other person in the house was her elderly father. It was my first home delivery and I was somewhat nervous, a state that apparently showed because the elderly man asked me gently if there was anything he could do to help. The only thing I could think of was a line out of a movie.

"Bring me lots of hot water and towels," I said.

He returned in a few moments with some newspapers as there were no spare towels in the house, and we placed these in reasonable positions to diminish the mess. About five minutes later he came back in with a kettle of very hot water. We looked at each other and I could not imagine what I would use it for. Sensing my uncertainty, he smiled and quietly asked if perhaps he should make some tea with this water. I nodded and went back to delivering the baby. Everything turned out fine and when it was all over we shared a cup of delicious tea.

Providing a coroner service was another of the many roles that physicians played on the Sunshine Coast, and for my first years with the partnership, while Al Swan functioned as the official

Red Nicholson was an entertainer as well as a fisherman, a true outdoorsman and valued friend and mentor.

coroner, I was his assistant. This meant that whenever there was a violent death such as a motor vehicle or logging accident or a drowning, we had to determine the cause of death by doing an autopsy, even in cases where the cause was obvious. My job was to perform the autopsy while Al conducted the inquest.

Since the hospital did not have a proper morgue and no funds to pay for an attendant to prepare the body after the autopsy was done, inquests were held at the funeral parlour where the undertaker could take over after the investigation. For the jury Al needed six loyal men "tried and true," plus one for a spare, which meant seven people had to be rounded up every time there was a coroner's inquest. The police would accomplish this by visiting the most popular Sechelt coffee shop at ten o'clock the morning after the death and an officer would point his finger at seven guys having coffee there. Invariably included were the mechanics from the two local service stations, as well as a couple of barbers. Once, having been warned that a violent death had occurred, these men saw the police officers approaching and tried to bolt out the back door only to be welcomed into the arms of another policeman who, with an appropriate mix of humour and authority, fingered them all for jury duty.

While most of the violent deaths on the coast were from motor vehicle and logging accidents, drowning deaths were also frequent and many of the victims were loggers travelling to or from the camps where they worked. For some inexplicable reason loggers were not necessarily good boaters and most treated the crewboat with the same indifference as they did the crummy used to transport land crews to logging sites. Few knew how to swim and even fewer knew anything about the mechanics of operating a boat or the inconsistent weather patterns that could transform a calm inlet into a deadly sea in a matter of minutes. Life jackets were seldom donned and weather warnings frequently ignored.

One such tragedy occurred on April 13, 1960, when six loggers left for home from their camp up Sechelt Inlet. It was late afternoon and a storm was already raging, but since it was only a fifteen-mile run, the men were sure they could make it. By eight o'clock they were reported missing, and the whole town turned out to search for their fifteen-foot open aluminum boat. Early the following morning it was discovered half-submerged, but the bodies of the six loggers were never found.

Many of these boating accidents could have been avoided if those involved had only listened to the advice of people who were more familiar with the temperamental nature of the local waters. Certainly this would have prevented the deaths of eight loggers who were returning to Garden Bay from Texada Island one stormy afternoon. The camp boss had called Red Nicholson to collect them in his water taxi. Red said he would come when the storm let up and advised that it was far too dangerous for them to go out in the camp boat. However, they did and none of them made it home; only four of the bodies were recovered, one of them unidentified.[16] When the undertaker, John Harvey, asked me for the name of someone who might recognize the unknown man, I brought Red Nicholson to the funeral parlour. Red found himself looking down at the body of the camp boss, and after naming him, he said, "You stupid bugger! I told you not to try it."

I was already thinking that such tragedies were just a way of life on this coast when one July night in 1960 off Gower Point the fish boat *Unimak* hit a scow and overturned. Air in the *Unimak's* hull kept it afloat and someone could be heard banging on the hull from inside. The *Princess of Vancouver*, a CPR boat full of passengers travelling from Nanaimo to Vancouver, was diverted to act as a breakwater while rescuers worked in increasingly rough water to attach lines from the *Brentwood*, a vessel with a tall mast and a derrick, to the overturned fishboat. Suddenly the *Brentwood's* mast snapped

Red Nicholson and Al Swan, two of my best friends—and mentors in fishing and medicine, respectively.

and before countermeasures could be taken, the *Unimak* rolled over and sank. The following day the boat was raised and towed to the beach where the bodies of two men and a woman were recovered.

As the summer of 1960 rolled into fall and winter into spring Bonnie and I fell more and more in love with the Sunshine Coast. Money was still tight as I struggled to pay off my student loans and the money we'd borrowed for our cross-Canada trip, but we were busy discovering the joys and challenges of parenthood, and besides, there were plenty of free activities to keep us busy. We loved to swim and fish and, we discovered, to garden, a skill we learned by trial and error and from vague memories of the techniques our parents used to produce the wonderful fruits and vegetables of our childhoods. Fortunately, this coast is peppered with avid gardeners who are eager to share cuttings and advice.

By this time we were averaging a hundred and twenty-five deliveries a year at the hospital in Garden Bay, so placentas were plentiful, and I got the idea of planting one under each of my tomato plants. I thought the resulting tomatoes were super delicious, but others were not so enthusiastic and were reluctant to eat them.

During these early years I was also becoming more and more familiar with my community of regular patients, partly due to what Al and I called our "Sunday Tea Rounds"—home visits to patients who could not make the long road trip to Garden Bay or even to our Sechelt clinic. The territory we covered ranged from Halfmoon Bay to Port Mellon and our calls would number from twenty to twenty-four on a typical day. Every little old lady we saw would offer us tea and cookies until we were saturated. It often happened that before I even got settled down in the house, the phone would ring and it would be a neighbour saying that she'd seen the doctor's car pull into the yard and could you send him over when he was finished. Sometimes I felt a bit like a Fuller Brush salesman.

The Sunshine Coast had a crank-style telephone system in those days, with operators who would transfer our calls. Often we gave the operator on duty a list of the places we would be visiting, but even if we didn't, these special women, such as Marg Burley and Barbara Aune, always seemed to know where we were. When someone asked for our number, they would say, "Well, I can give you the number, but the doctor isn't at home—though I think I know where he is." She would then track us down and pass on the message.

One of the regulars on my tea rounds was a Mrs. B. Her husband, Charlie, was a quiet, elderly Swede, but in his younger days he had been a miner and prospector in the Yukon. In July 1924 he had staked the rich Elsa claim, but his most legendary success came the following May when he was out grouse hunting nearby. He took a shot at a grouse but only wounded it and it flew off into the buckbrush. He followed but quickly forgot about the bird when he discovered surface ore that would later assay at three thousand ounces of silver per ton. This became the Lucky Strike claim. Over the next thirty years he made and lost several fortunes, but in 1954 after his health deteriorated, he retired to a seaside cottage near Roberts Creek with his third wife.

This lady had come into his life after his story was written up in the *Vancouver Sun*. She had been wealthy herself at one time but had squandered it on the good life and hoped to live it again on Charlie's money. Alas, she discovered after marrying him that he had little money left, having given it to his niece Elsa when he discovered this rich lady was interested in him, and she made his life hell, accusing him of deceiving her. He stuck it out stoically, although she was very high maintenance and I was often called to visit her on my Sunday Tea Rounds. After her death in 1963 he returned to his home town in Sweden where he died in October 1970.[17]

An unusual side effect of these tea rounds was a friendship that developed with retired siblings Dorothy and Norman Lightfoot. Dorothy, a lifelong spinster, had been summoned from England in 1912 to join her family in Vancouver, but she had been ordered not to sail on the *Titanic* because it was, according to her aunt, an "evil ship." And she didn't. After her parents died, Dorothy was required to look after her brother Norman, whose wife and two daughters had left him to join the flock of the American evangelist "Father" Divine, who founded the International Peace Mission and claimed to be God.

Dorothy and Norman required a lot of attention, and after a number of years they announced one day that they wanted to sell their cottage in Roberts Creek, buy a trailer and move it onto our acreage in Selma Park. This would make it easier for me to attend to their needs, and besides, Bonnie, whom they both liked very much, could provide them with suppers! For some years after that, our kids would hike through the forest to their trailer with their evening meals.

Another service we provided in the community was the medical care of animals, both big and small. I usually couldn't tell what was wrong with them, but if they seemed to be having any kind of chest trouble, I gave them both penicillin and digitalis in case it was either a lung infection or heart failure. Since there was no SPCA on the coast, we also inadvertently became an animal euthanasia service. One day two little old ladies asked me to come to their house to end the life of their old poodle who was blind, deaf, arthritic and in pain. To ease his death, I gave the dog a shot of morphine, the last that I had in my bag. I thought it would be enough, and after I had administered the shot, the dog lay on the couch with the ladies weeping and wailing around him. I placed my hand on his chest, feeling his heart beating slower and slower and his respirations diminishing to about one every thirty seconds. Then gradually it became clear to me that he was starting to breathe once every twenty seconds and that he wasn't going to die. At that moment, between sobs over what she thought was her dead poodle, one of the ladies asked if I she could do anything for me.

"Oh, yes!" I said. "I could sure use a cup of tea."

As I hoped would happen, both ladies bounded into the kitchen. I looked at the dog who was obviously waking up and did what I had to do.

When another lady from Roberts Creek called me to put her dog down, I fortunately had enough morphine to do the job properly. After it was over, I noticed that the woman, who was very obese, didn't look so well. "When was the last time you saw a doctor?" I asked.

"Haven't seen a doctor in forty years," she said.

"Well, why don't you just let me check your blood pressure?" I said, and when she agreed, I brought out my gear. Her pressure was sky high. "You should come into the office and have a complete checkup," I told her. She promised that she would. Later that morning she went to church, then came home and buried her dog. Afterwards she had a nap and died during her sleep. I have always thought that she must have known something was going to happen to her and wanted her dog looked after.

Dogs, however, were not the only animals we treated. One day a man from Pender Harbour phoned me and said his horse had broken his leg and could I do something for him. I hauled our old portable x-ray machine to his farm, but while I was in the process of x-raying the horse's leg, I blew the tube on the machine. As it turned out, the leg was broken. Since I could do nothing for the horse, and the man had to put it down, he said that he didn't think doctors should charge for animal care and refused to pay for the visit. A new tube would cost $300, but as Al Swan noted later, the incident did force us to get a new unit.

Our lobbying for a new hospital continued, but it was slowed by both provincial bureaucracy and local bickering over where the new facility should be located. On January 19, 1961, a magnificent donation by the Sechelt Indian Band of eleven acres of land across from the residential school settled that issue, but when it was followed by an announcement from the government that only one Sunshine Coast hospital would be funded, a new wave of protests was started by the good citizens of Garden Bay. Back in 1930 many of them had volunteered labour or materials for the construction of the old building, and all of them had supported the hospital financially for the past thirty-one years. The notion that it would now be taken from them was nothing short of betrayal. Heading the protest was Al Lloyd, a former chair of the hospital society and the owner of Lloyd's General Store in Garden Bay, and during the time that I was in Pender Harbour we were close friends. He had initially led the fight to get a second hospital on the coast, but now he and other Garden Bay residents began fighting just as hard to keep the original building operating. Claiming that the people of Pender

Al Lloyd had initially led the fight to open a new hospital on the Sunshine Coast, but with the announcement that only one hospital would be funded, he and other Garden Bay residents began fighting just as hard to keep the original building operating.

Harbour didn't understand what they were voting for when they approved the referendum, Al made a motion to renovate and modernize the old building instead of building a new one. Fortunately, his motion was defeated. [18]

While this squabbling was going on, the hospital staff and doctors continued to provide the best care they could. For me, that task came with surprising bits of humour, as was the case with one women whose husband was dying of prostate cancer. My hospital training had been completed in urban areas where there was always a system in place to deal with death—an ambulance delivered the body to the hospital where the person was pronounced dead and sent down to the morgue. It didn't work quite that way on the Sunshine Coast, so I wasn't surprised one March morning in 1961 when I received a call at four in the morning.

"Tom's dead," the woman said.

I was instantly awake and filled with concern. "Okay, I'll come right over and see him."

"Oh, you don't need to bother doing that," she reassured me. "I just wanted to know if I should turn the heat off in the house so the body won't smell by morning."

A few weeks later a fellow appeared in my office. A bachelor, he had come by boat from Doriston, up Sechelt Inlet, where he had lived with his parents and brother since their arrival from Sweden in 1924.[19] I had flown there on several occasions to treat his elderly mother. This man was at least six feet tall, a slow-moving, slow-talking fellow who seldom started conversations—except on this occasion. He said, "I brought Mudder."

I looked beyond the door, but there was no one with him. "Where is she?"

"In the boat."

"Oh. Well, I'll come down and have a look," I said, rising from my desk.

The man held up his hand. "She's dead."

After several more questions I determined that the man and his brother had put their mother's body in a coffin and brought her to Sechelt along with some spades. Apparently she didn't want to be buried in the wilderness, but they couldn't afford an undertaker so he wanted to know where they could bury her. John Harvey, the local undertaker, wasn't amused, but after some bureaucratic wrangling she was finally laid to rest in the local cemetery.

There were times, however, when death fooled us. Art was a wizened old man who lived deep in the bush at the upper end of Tyson Road. His home was a tarpaper shack that had a mud floor covered with cardboard. He surfaced only when absolutely necessary, always caked in a permanent armour of grunge, which I am sure is what kept the bacteria out, and he did not smell too pretty.

One day when our waiting room was jammed with patients, Arthur appeared in my office with the most dreadfully infected ingrown toenail. Deciding that the only thing to do was to remove the toenail, I laid him up on the table in the surgery and injected the local anaesthetic. Although Arthur was probably eighty-five at this time, I'm not sure that he had ever had a local anaesthetic before, and he passed right out on me. For all I knew he was dead. I called out to our receptionist, Margaret Bolderson, to track down Al Swan, and a few minutes later Al dashed into the room to help. He took one look at my patient, and although he also decided that the man was dead, we initiated a resuscitative manoeuvre and brought him around.

Later over coffee Al and I compared notes about this event. Certain that Arthur was dead, I had been worried about getting him out of the clinic without taking him through the waiting room and obviously upsetting a few people. *Maybe we can lower him through the window to the ground*, I had thought. At the same time Al had been working on a similar scenario, only his plan was to put Arthur in the small darkroom where we developed our x-rays and leave him there for the rest of the day. Fortunately, neither solution was necessary.

There were other times when being so familiar with the community made it difficult for me to deny my patients treatments that skirted the edge of professionalism. Harry was an old, semi-invalid ex-logger with a strange weakness and paresthesia from his waist down, which he claimed was the result of standing in cold water in the lakes of northern Ontario. One day he came to me with a story about a miraculous injection called "H-3" from Hungary.

"It's called novocaine, Doc, and it restores you!"

We used novocaine in our practice as a local anaesthetic, but I had never heard of it being used in this way. "It won't work, Harry."

"We can try it, can't we?" he pleaded.

Since it was harmless, I relented and gave him a ten-cc shot in his buttock, and then once a week as I passed through Halfmoon Bay on my way to the hospital, I would give him another shot. Each time he told me how much better he was feeling. Then one day he told me he had just seen an "old friend," and for the first time in many years he had experienced an erection. Harry was so excited by this that he told his buddies, and the next week they were all in his shack waiting to get their shots as well. Fortunately, the College of Physicians and Surgeons had somehow heard about what I was doing and ordered me to stop or face disciplinary action. It was one time when our bureaucracy worked and got me out of a very touchy situation.

Home visits were often complicated by the absence of the supplies and equipment readily available during office consultations. One dark and stormy night I visited an elderly woman in Roberts Creek who needed to have her pessary changed. She had developed a major uterine prolapse and an inflatable donut-shaped pessary had been inserted into her vagina to keep the uterus in place. Since the best light in the house was in the living room, I used the couch as a treatment table, positioning the woman on her back with her legs wide apart and her knees bent. Her husband discreetly left the room while I removed the old device and inserted a new, uninflated pessary. Connected to it and hanging out of her vagina was a short tube with a metal adapter to which a squeeze mechanism could be attached to inflate the device. To my horror, I realized I had not brought the inflater. Not wishing to make a second visit, I instinctively bent down and blew into the free end of the tube, but it didn't work. I straightened up from what, in retrospect, was a very compromising position just as the woman's husband came in with a cup of tea and a plate of cookies. Neither he nor my patient ever commented on this new approach to her treatment, but it was one I never attempted again.

Although I had been taught all about illness, I had received no training in wellness or counselling, but there were many times when I was called upon to dispense advice as a counsellor rather than a doctor. The first of these occasions occurred very early in my career. After I removed a parotid tumour from a forty-year-old man, the doctors at the BC Cancer Clinic told him the operation for this type of cancer was not curative and that chemo or radiation therapy would be ineffective. In short, he was sent home to die.

In my office we discussed his options.

"What would you do?" he asked.

After a few moments of reflection, I said, "I would sell my business and spend all my money travelling around the world."

The man nodded, thanked me and left the office. I heard a few months later that he had sold his motel business and he and his wife had disappeared.

Some twenty-five years later a man in his late sixties sat in my office grinning at me. I didn't recognize him until he showed me the scar near his ear.

"How could this be?" I asked, scarcely able to believe what I was seeing.

"Well, I followed your advice, Doctor," he said then related how he had spent all of his money travelling with his wife. After five years he was broke but still alive and had gone back to work. Now he was on welfare but still hanging in there.

I remarked that I had obviously given him bad advice, but he shook his head.

"On the contrary," he said. "It was the best advice in the world! I just dropped in to thank you."

In September 1961, Bonnie was admitted to the hospital for another Caesarean section ten days earlier than planned because the baby was showing signs of distress. Tom Masterson did the surgery, while Al Swan handled the anaesthesia, but for some reason the spinal anaesthetic didn't do the job it was supposed to, and Bonnie could feel a lot more than just tugs and pulls. As soon as the baby was detached from the umbilical cord, a regular anaesthetic was administered, and our second daughter, Carla, was born with no other complications. Bonnie chose her name not realizing that at that moment Hurricane Carla was churning its way across the Gulf of Mexico towards Texas.

One dark evening later that fall as I was driving up Rat Portage Hill in Roberts Creek, I had to brake suddenly to avoid hitting a huge, hairy, two-legged creature crossing the road. I was twenty-eight years of age at the time with excellent vision and a reasonably sound mind, and although I saw the animal for less than ten seconds, I was certain that it was the legendary Big Foot. Thoroughly shaken, I continued on my way to Gibsons, but the next day I told Al Swan about my encounter. "I'm absolutely sure it was a sasquatch!" I said.

"Eric," he cautioned, "I don't think you should tell anybody else about this. Think of the negative publicity such a story would generate and the damage it would do to your credibility."

As usual, he gave good advice. Who would want to go to a doctor who saw sasquatches?

That year my parents came from Alberta to share Christmas with us. My father had never said much about my chosen profession, but I knew he still harboured a resentment towards doctors because of the debts he had incurred for our family's medical care. In the early morning hours of Christmas Eve I received a call from a patient who lived on a farm in Gibsons. He said his mother was suffering from severe stomach pains and would I come to see her. Without waking any of my family, I slipped out and drove the twenty-five kilometres to the man's home, but when I got to the house, he met me at the door and said his mother was no longer in pain, that they didn't need me to see her, and therefore, they would not be expecting a bill from me.

Knowing it was useless to argue, I quietly turned around and went home. It was just after four when I walked into the kitchen and there were my mother and dad giving Carla her bottle. They looked up at me in amazement.

"Where have you been?" Dad asked.

"I was on a house call," I said, "and now I'm going back to bed."

As I left the kitchen I heard Dad say to Mum, "You know, maybe doctors do earn their money."

I noticed that his attitude towards my profession mellowed a little after that.

As busy as we were, the friendship between Al Swan and myself never wavered, although we did occasionally challenge one another. Early in our acquaintance Al had told me that he could recall everything that he read. A short time later an elderly couple came into my office, and after telling me that they had just been to England, they showed me a ruler they had brought back as a souvenir. Printed on the back were the names of all thirty-six British monarchs.

"Mind if I borrow this for a moment?" I asked the couple, and after they shook their heads, I walked over to Al's office.

"Can you give me the names of all the British monarchs?" I asked him.

"Starting with the Celts or the Normans?" he asked, then proceeded to name each one. He got them all right.

Although Al Swan was the most conscientious doctor God ever created, unfortunately he didn't handle the stress associated with our work as well as Walter and I did. He couldn't just go home and forget it. If he had a patient who was in a really tough situation or a treatment that hadn't turned out well, it just bothered the heck out of him and he couldn't get the case out of his head. The controversy surrounding the new hospital wasn't helping either because many of the Pender Harbour people protesting the hospital's move to Sechelt, including Al Lloyd, were friends of long standing. It was of some help in May 1962 when Sunshine Coast residents voted 84.2 percent in favour of a referendum to provide funds to help cover the cost of building the hospital, but by then Al was on sabbatical in Honolulu.[20]

After being accepted into the surgical residency program at the The Queen's Medical Center in Oahu, Al had left on the first of our sabbaticals, initiating a professional development program that in time made our group the envy of other medical practices in the province. For Walter and me his absence revealed the full extent of his workload, for while Al was involved with the hospital building committee as well as carrying out all of the house calls, hospital rounds and on-call duties that we did, on his days off he and Rosa would also take their children by boat up Jervis Inlet to Vancouver Bay where he held informal clinics at the logging camp there. It is no wonder that in later years he often maintained that our sabbatical program literally saved his life.

"Although the life of a surgical resident is a hard one," he said in a 2002 oral history, "it was like a piece of cake compared to being home. It was that easy."[21]

To cope with his absence, Walter and I began to search for another partner. By this time there were a lot of positions available and doctors were becoming hard to find, so we had to give incentives even to get them to come to see us. We paid for one doctor to fly out from Winnipeg for an interview, but clearly he just wanted a holiday because he never even said thank

Just under six feet tall, Dr. Jim Hobson was a quiet, gutsy guy and a conscientious, reliable physician. With his addition to our team, we were able to establish a clinic in Gibsons.

The late Dr. Frederick Inglis had been the Sunshine Coast's very first doctor, and Dr. Hugh Inglis followed in his father's footsteps. Hugh joined our clinic as an associate, and we opened for business on December 18, 1962.

you. Thus, when we found Jim Hobson, we wanted to do everything we could to ensure that he stayed.

Around the same age as Al and Walter, Jim came from Vancouver Island. Just under six feet tall, he was a quiet, gutsy guy and a conscientious, reliable physician. With his addition to our team, we were able to establish a clinic in Gibsons at the intersection of School and Gower Point roads. A former post office, the building was now owned by Doctor Hugh Inglis who had renovated the upper floor for use as a medical clinic. Hugh's father, the late Frederick Inglis, the Sunshine Coast's first doctor, had arrived in 1913 and had provided medical care for people from Pender Harbour to Port Mellon until he retired in 1945. Hugh's practice had been in Stonehurst, the family home directly across from us that his father had built in 1914, but now he joined our clinic as an associate, and we opened for business on December 18, 1962. To provide relief coverage, it was decided that I would spend one day a week at this clinic.[22]

Dwight Johnson, another physician practising in Gibsons, worked from his house on Seaview Road. He and his wife had been missionaries in the Orient until they retired to the coast in 1959.[23] Although he had privileges at the hospital and did some minor surgeries, such as tonsillectomies, Dwight mainly kept to himself so I never saw very much of him.

While most of Jim Hobson's time was spent in the clinic, he did go up to Garden Bay to deliver his maternity cases, and one morning at about two o'clock he received a message that one of his patients was at the hospital and about to deliver. About ten minutes later the baby was born, but when the nurse tried to call him back, she was told that Jim had already left home. Since Bonnie and I now lived by the highway in West Sechelt, the nurse called me and asked if I would go out and stand by the side of the road. When Jim came by I was to flag him down so he would not have to go all the way to Garden Bay. I grumbled, but since we couldn't afford to lose Jim's services, I did as they requested, but when I told Jim he was no longer needed, he decided he would go to the hospital anyway just to make sure his patient was alright.

During Al's absence, Walter Burtnick began putting in a few days a week to help me at the Sechelt clinic. One day on our coffee break he asked me what I was planning to do next, and I explained that a lady was in the x-ray room waiting to have a tooth pulled. When I mentioned her name, Walt's expression grew frantic.

"Don't let her take her shoes off!" he warned.

As soon as I stepped into the little, windowless room I knew what he meant. The lady *had* taken her shoes off and the stench hit me like a stone wall. The poor lady couldn't help it, but the smell was awful—it was so bad that I had to go outside, hyperventilate, return just long enough to freeze the area around the tooth and then escape back into the hallway until it was time to do the extraction.

That summer pilot Fred Ritter flew me to a fishing lodge at Clowhom Falls to make a house call. The caretaker's wife had radio-phoned that her husband was sick and needed a doctor. Unfortunately when I arrived, the man was already dead. It was now twilight and the pilot said we only had time to make one flight back to Sechelt before dark, and since it was a small aircraft, there was room for only one more passenger. I suggested to the woman that she should fly out with us.

"No," she said, "take my husband out and come back for me in the morning."

Consequently, Fred and I carried the man down to the beach and trundled him into the back seat of the plane, strapping him in with the seatbelt. This made Fred awfully uncomfortable, and as he was flying the plane, he kept looking nervously over his right shoulder. Meanwhile, I used Fred's radio phone to call the Tyee office in Sechelt and ask them to have a hearse awaiting us when we got there.

"Surely you mean an ambulance," said Shirley Summerfield, the Tyee clerk.

"No, I mean hearse," I repeated.

There was a long pause and then she said, "You mean . . ."

After a further pause, I said, "That's right. He's dead."

Knowing that we had the small plane, she asked, "But where is he?"

"Sitting in the back seat, looking over our shoulders and enjoying the flight!"

Obviously this was a bit too much for them to handle because, when we got to Porpoise Bay, there was no one in the office—just a message saying that the hearse would be there shortly.

Al Swan's sabbatical also meant that I was appointed coroner by the attorney general, and Walter, as my assistant, now did the autopsies. One of the first cases we handled together occurred in July. A twenty-five-year-old man who lived in Wilson Creek had been hosting a big party when, having had a bit too much to drink, he had felt insulted by something that was said and stomped out the door. The next thing anybody knew he had poked his head through the open window from outside and shouted that he had shot himself. Everyone was playing cards and drinking beer, and because they thought he was just drunk, most of them ignored him. One guest, however, decided to phone me just in case. When I arrived, I found the man wandering around outside with a .22 rifle in his hand.

"I shot myself!" he said, slurring the words.

"Where?" I asked, seeing no visible signs of a wound. He pointed right to his heart, but though I examined his shirt, I still could not see a wound. "Show me how you did it," I instructed, whereupon he stuck the rifle into his shirt pocket, then levelled the gun off.

"Like this," he said.

I looked into his shirt pocket and sure enough, there was a burn hole through the inside fabric, and when he took off his shirt I found a small bullet wound underneath his left nipple. Realizing that he was in shock rather than just drunk, I called for an ambulance, then told his family and friends that I was taking him to the hospital in Garden Bay. As the young man was still walking and talking, they didn't believe anything serious had happened, and guffawing they called out, "Have fun, Doc!" and went back to partying.

By the time we got to the main intersection in Sechelt, the man's heart had stopped and I was unable to resuscitate him. The autopsy that Walter did the next day showed that the bullet had actually hit a rib and ricocheted in such a way that it had gone along the inside of the lower rib all the way to his right side where it penetrated the liver. The bullet had missed his heart, but he had hemorrhaged to death very slowly through the small wound in his liver.

Another difficult case that year was when we were called in to treat a young man who had been critically injured in a motor vehicle accident. His father was called to the bedside because the young man was literally dying on us. As we worked frantically to save his son, the father fainted, but we had no time to pay any attention to him. Only after we had stabilized our patient could we turn to deal with the man on the floor. To our horror he was dead, having suffered a massive heart attack.

Our coastal emergencies did not always occur up the

Sunshine Coast's northern inlets. Some came from Howe Sound, and these included a call I received from the Gibsons RCMP detachment to advise that there was an injured man at Centre Bay on Gambier Island who needed medical attention. They took me in their police boat, and after docking, we had to climb up a hill to where the patient lay shaded by a large fir tree. His multiple injuries were so severe and painful that I started him on morphine right away, and as soon as he was stabilized, we carried him by stretcher down to the boat and headed for Horseshoe Bay. I had a lot of morphine with me and kept giving him more whenever he showed signs of pain, and for the most part he seemed quite comfortable. Thus, I was surprised when he asked, "Hey Doc, have you got an aspirin? I have a terrible headache."

While this man was grateful for my services, there were some patients who refused to acknowledge that the treatment I administered did them any good at all. Elizabeth was a really bad asthmatic who lived in Roberts Creek. Often her husband would call me around two in the morning to say that his wife needed a shot, a combination of adrenalin, a bronchial relaxant and a steroid preparation, which gave her almost immediate relief. However, Elizabeth was a Christian Scientist who believed in reflexology and on more than one occasion she would refuse the injection, even though she was close to her dying breath.

Wearily I would trundle off home, only to be roused again two hours later by the phone ringing. "The wife will have that shot now," her husband would say, and I would dutifully drive back to the Creek and give her the injection. This always made her feel so much better that she'd head for the first ferry to Vancouver to see her reflexologist, to whom she gave all the credit for her cure.

Having a keen interest in alternate forms of medicine, I once asked an elderly Native shaman how her people handled various illnesses, such as paralysis. The shaman, who was a member of the *Tsonai* sept of the *Shishalh* nation who lived at

Deserted Bay, said that they would come all the way down to Sechelt to collect mud from Porpoise Bay, and for weeks the patient would be immersed in a mud bath several times a day.

"Did it work?" I asked the shaman.

She gave a slow grin. "Sometimes," she said.

In 1984 the mud of Porpoise Bay attracted a German couple who added an annex to Rockwood Lodge and opened it as the Western Moorbad Resort, featuring a fairly sophisticated mud bath facility. Although their research had convinced them of the healing properties of the local mud, the venture failed.

Another alternate medical treatment I was exposed to was moxibustion, which was used by Tom Ono's sister, Bessie Baba. In this traditional Asian remedy, a small quantity of combustible material was placed on the skin and set alight, causing a painful burn blister designed to serve as a counterirritant. It was used to combat many ailments. When it didn't work, I was called in.

Without Al to share the driving, my trips to Garden Bay seemed to last longer and to be more frequent. On one glorious twenty-four-hour day of being on call, I made the trip from Sechelt five times. The last call was in response to a car accident and fortunately, because they needed a surgeon immediately, I was flown in by helicopter. It was dark before all of the accident victims had been cared for, and I gratefully accepted RCMP Constable Bob Selwood's offer to drive me home. We had almost reached Kleindale when we met a car that was weaving all over the road, crossing so far into our lane that we barely avoided an accident.

"You in a great hurry to get to Sechelt, Doc?" Bob asked.

"Not that much," I said.

He turned around on the highway and, with siren blaring, we chased after the car. When it stopped, he marched over to the driver's side and ordered the woman at the wheel to step out where he told her to walk the white line. It was obvious that she was very drunk, and as she staggered down the white line, the other five occupants of the car focussed their full attention on her. But they all stared at Bob in amazement when he thanked her very kindly and wished them all a pleasant evening. He then marched back to the police car. As he turned the car around and headed back to Sechelt, I said, "You're letting them go?"

With a big grin, he opened his hand and showed me the car keys that he had surreptitiously removed.

"Takes them off the road and saves me a lot of paperwork," he said.

I thought it was rather appropriate—if somewhat rough—justice.

The longer I stayed on the Sunshine Coast, the more of its unique characters I was able to meet. Among these was the Solberg family. Herman and Olga had emigrated from Norway in 1926 and settled at Four Mile Point two years later. At that time there was no road to their homestead and the family

Minnie Solberg, the "Cougar Lady," could barely read but was an expert at hunting and wilderness survival. She was the watchman at Jackson's logging camp in Deserted Bay.

lived a semi-isolated existence. Although their two daughters, Minnie and Bergliot (Bergie) received rudimentary schooling by correspondence, they could barely read and write and had few social skills. They were, however, experts at hunting and wilderness survival, and they worked either as whistle punks for logging outfits or as camp watchers.

Herman became a high-maintenance patient in his later years, and his daughters were very solicitous. On several occasions he complained that he had "bad blood" in his leg and wanted me to drain it. His actual problem was varicose veins, but knowing that it was futile to argue with him, I applied a tourniquet to the leg until the vein bulged, and then aspirated twenty cc's of very dark blood. He and his daughters ooh-ed and ah-ed about this "terrible" blood, and he left smiling and feeling much better.

One beautifully sunny Friday afternoon at the end of August, a fifty-four-year-old man named Tom came into the Sechelt clinic. He was bruised all over and I suspected the worst. When a quick blood test confirmed the presence of acute leukemia, I told him that he must go to Vancouver immediately. As he was not feeling that bad, he questioned this decision, but I explained that it was of vital importance that he begin treatments immediately. Still, it wasn't until he heard me talking to Dr. Karjala in Vancouver, who said he would start the treatment that night at St. Paul's Hospital, that the man suddenly began to realize his situation was serious. Since he did not have a car and his wife was in Vancouver, I elected to drive him to the ferry.

It was after five-thirty when we left Sechelt, and because the next ferry was scheduled to leave in one hour, I thought we would arrive in plenty of time. I was surprised and dismayed when we pulled up to the toll booth to see the ferry pulling away from the dock. A number of cars had been left behind because it had been totally jammed. When I asked why it was leaving five minutes before its scheduled departure, the booth attendant, Sylvia Spain, who was a patient of mine, said, "Eric, this is the four-thirty ferry. It's late."

"But I've got a deathly sick man here!" I said. "He needs emergency treatment this evening. Everything is set up for him at St. Paul's Hospital."

Spurred by the urgency in my voice, Sylvia contacted the ferry captain, Alan White, who was also one of my patients, and after explaining the situation, handed me the phone.

"Eric," Captain White said, "if you'll back me up with management, I'll bring the ferry back and pick up your patient."

As soon as I agreed, he ordered the crew to turn the boat around and made an announcement over the public address system, explaining that they were returning to the dock to pick up a critically ill man. At once people began crowding the rails looking down to see the ambulance board the ferry. Instead, they saw my patient jauntily saunter onto the ferry smoking his cigarette and waving at some friends. Alan White phoned me that evening and said for sure this was going to cost him his job because the man had certainly not looked like a critical case to him. However, within a week I could write to the BC Ferry Authority exonerating the captain because my patient died just two days after being admitted to the hospital.

By 1963 I had a few home deliveries under my belt, but none of them had prepared me for the delivery of a patient's second child in Gibsons. I had delivered her previous baby in the Garden Bay Hospital, and it had been a generally bad experience for her since it had included a transverse arrest of the baby that required a complicated forceps delivery. She was determined to have this baby at home, but he was also in a transverse arrest position. She was in labour for three days— hard at it until she became exhausted and then it would stop for a while. I went to see her each day but she refused to go to the hospital. On the third day I arrived with the forceps, and then with the help of two public health nurses and Dr. Hugh

Inglis, who was very experienced with home deliveries, we set to work. The patient remembers us pushing and pulling but we finally reached a happy conclusion. During this whole process her husband was never in sight. He stayed in his road grader by day and in the basement by night.

In the late spring of 1963 Al Swan returned from his sabbatical in Hawaii, taking up his practice with renewed enthusiasm and providing me with much needed help in the operating room. One of our cases, however, was not exactly the kind of surgery that either of us had trained for. There was still no vet in the community, so when Vern Richter's large German shepherd dog fell ill, he brought him to our clinic. The dog had such a huge tumour in his neck that he could not keep his head up, and since both Al and I would be required to perform the operation to remove it, we enlisted Vern as the anaesthetist, instructing him to inject two cc's of Pentathol every time we told him to give the dog a booster. Everything went fine until the dog started to move.

"Oh-oh," Al said. "Vern, give him a booster!"

The urgency in Al's voice coupled with the consternation on our faces caused Vern to panic, and he gave the dog the whole twenty cc's of Pentathol at once. This, of course, created a non-breathing dog, and we were now stuck because we didn't even have an Am-bu bag to resuscitate him. Al and I looked at each other and then at Vern who was breaking down in tears, pulling at his scant hair and chastising himself.

Fortunately, we had already intubated the dog so there was a long endotracheal tube sticking out of its mouth, and I pointed to it and told Vern, "You'll have to give him mouth-to-mouth resuscitation through that tube." So while we soldiered on with the surgery, Vern breathed into the tube until the overdose wore off. The surgery was a success and the dog lived for several more years. Curious about the growth, we sent the specimen to St. Paul's Hospital under the name R. Richter. The pathologist there, Dr. Rutherford, came back with a rare diagnosis but added, "The *dog* should do just fine." We could never figure out how he knew.

Most of the patients who came to our clinics had legitimate complaints, but occasionally we encountered a scammer. One such patient had been milking the Worker's Compensation system for a long time, but I could never prove that his injured back was not as bad as he claimed it to be. Then, while walking along the beach one day, I came around a corner and found him cutting up a bunch of firewood and pitching huge blocks as far as he could towards his truck. I watched as he bent down, picked up a big chunk and in one smooth, twisting motion tossed it to a pile thirty feet away. It was clear that there was nothing wrong with his back, and when I walked up to him and said hello, he had enough of a sense of humour to look at me and grin.

"Well, I guess I'll be back at work on Monday," he said.

"You sure will," I responded.

Al Swan had a similar patient who had hoodwinked him for an equal length of time until he caught the guy at a community dance jiving like he'd never seen anyone jive before. He even won the limbo contest, and as he walked up to claim his award, he saw Al in the crowd and realized that his back injury claim had come to an end.

Shortly after Al's return I woke one Sunday morning with severe abdominal pain. I was on call at that time and after dealing with two patients over the phone, I told Bonnie, "You know, I'm sicker than these people who want me to come visit them!"

It didn't take me forever to diagnose my problem as appendicitis, and I quickly rousted out Al Swan and Jim Hobson who drove me to the hospital and removed my appendix. I was still recovering on Tuesday morning when they had a problem in the operating room, and I had to get out of bed to help sort it out. When the crisis was over, I decided that if I was well enough to do surgery, I was certainly well enough to go home.

My three-week recovery period gave me lots of time to think about my career. Becoming a fully qualified surgeon required four years of surgical residency, and when I had completed my first year at San Diego, I had planned to return one day to complete the final three. Since I was next in line for a sabbatical, I decided this was a good time to resume my training, and I began to investigate surgical residency programs at various hospitals. One day I was speaking of this to Harry Morris, a GP who had recently joined our practice. Harry had been an immigration doctor in Germany in the 1950s and he was good friends with a surgeon in the Rhine area.

"Why don't you go to Germany?" he asked. "You speak German."

"That sounds like a good idea," I agreed.

"Good," he said, "I will set you up with a friend of mine who is a professor of surgery at the *Städtisches Krankenhaus* in Ludwigshafen."

He did exactly that and within weeks Bonnie and I were making preparations to vacate our home and transport ourselves and our two young daughters to Germany.

CHAPTER 4

A German Cut-Up

With our two small daughters in tow, Bonnie and I left Sechelt in early May 1963 and once again drove eastward across the prairies, visiting with relatives along the way. In Montreal we boarded a train for New York where we had a berth on a ship bound for Rotterdam. From this port we took another train to Ludwigshafen. The next day, with Bonnie and the children safely ensconced in a hotel, I made my way to the state hospital, taking time along the way to study this city that was to be our home for the next twelve months.

Lugwigshafen was one of the most severely bombed cities in Germany during World War II, partly because of its immense chemical and munitions factories. It is also located just across the Rhine from the city of Manheim where the junction of the Rhine and Neckar rivers made both cities an easy target for the Allied bombers. As a consequence, more than fifty percent of the buildings in Lugwigshafen were destroyed. After the war a massive reconstruction project was initiated and by 1963, when we arrived, it had become one of the most modern metropolitan centres in Europe, with gleaming new tower blocks, raised highways and other architectural marvels.

The state hospital was the largest medical facility in the

area as well as the burn and trauma centre for the region. Of the fifteen hundred beds available, three hundred and thirty were in the surgical department. I had never seen such a huge operating centre. Everything was state-of-the-art, the latest and the best, and everyone on staff was smart and well-trained.

With some difficulty I found my way to the surgical ward where I met Professor Heinz Gelbke. About six feet tall, he was an aristocratic-looking man with a patrician nose. Although he had an aura about him that seemed to say, "I'm Professor Gelbke, and you're not," he was a brilliant surgeon and a very capable man, who was always very fair. That morning he introduced me to the eighteen residents with whom I would be training, and since I spoke fluent German, I thought that I blended in with this crowd. I was rather deflated when one of the female residents told me later, "We knew right away that you were North American. Just by your demeanour, by the way you looked and carried yourself, we could tell you weren't German."

After a short discussion of what I might expect from the program, the professor said, "You go now to the administration office and they will get all your details so you can be on the payroll."

I did as I was told and met the administration officer, who immediately checked her files. "Good," she said. "You're on the list." With some relief I handed her my paperwork, but as I turned to leave, she stopped me. "You do not have a *Permission to Stay*, Herr Paetkau. It is required before I can pay you."

"Oh? And where do I go for that?" I asked.

She directed me to the appropriate office where I was greeted by a man of about my own age. I told him my story and showed him my contract with the hospital. "I just need you to sign a *Permission to Stay* in Germany for one year," I said.

He was about to fill out this form when he suddenly stopped. "Before I can give you that I must see your *Permission to Work* form," he said.

This time I was directed to a building several blocks away where an obliging young man filled out yet another form. He raised his pen to sign it, then paused and shook his head. "Before I can give you a *Permission to Work,* you need to show me your *Permission to Stay* form."

"Oh-oh," I said. "I've been there already. They say they can't give it to me until I have the *Permission to Work* form."

We stared at each other, locked in an impasse that neither of us knew how to breach. Finally he asked, "Well, what would you do in Canada?"

"If I were you? I'd just sign it and send me on my way."

"But," he said, "this is Germany. I don't know if I can do that."

"Okay," I said. "Get on the phone. Call your counterpart at the other office and both of you sign at the same time."

He laughed and picked up the phone. "He's here," he said after an explanation. "I'll sign if you'll sign." And that was it.

Our housing arrangements proved to be almost as complicated as my entry into the ranks of Germany's work force. At first we rented a basement apartment in the city, but neither Bonnie nor I liked it. After two weeks we found a place that was actually closer to the hospital, just along the riverbank and outside a small village. When we arrived with our luggage, we were told that we had to secure a *Permission to Leave* from the police in our old jurisdiction and *Permission to Stay* from the police in the new jurisdiction. Only when this was accomplished were we allowed to move into our new home.

As in Canada, a surgical residency in Germany was a four-year program, but there was a slightly different twist. Each year the residents were expected to learn procedures that grew more and more complex. The resident's goal at the end of the final year was to become a chief resident, and here a problem arose because only two of the eighteen residents could be selected for this position. The others went into country hospitals and became practising surgeons in rural areas. The chief residents stayed until they obtained a city hospital appointment, which was determined by whatever government was in power. If you were a Christian Democrat and the government in power was Christian Democrat, your chances for getting that appointment were better than the next guy.

I was now in my second year of surgery, which meant I would receive a certain standard of teaching, but Professor Gelbke, knowing that I was only going to be there for one year and being very proud to have a Canadian surgeon train under him, would frequently ask me, "What do you want to learn?" Each time he asked, I would suggest a different procedure, such as a colon resection, a surgery I normally would not learn until the fourth year, and the professor would turn to his chief resident and say, "You make sure he gets to do bowel surgery." So I jumped the queue, as it were.

My group was made up of five residents, and I became really good friends with one of them and got along with two more. The fifth member of our team, however, didn't like the idea that I was getting preferential treatment. A graduate from Heidelberg University, he was a German nationalist and had a duelling scar on his face. No matter how often I explained to this man that I was only there for one year and would not be competing with him, the privileges I was receiving still rankled him.

"Why can't I learn to do some of those major procedures?" he complained repeatedly.

Exasperated by his continuous whining, I turned on him one day and said, "If you don't shut up, I'm going to buy this hospital and fire you!"

He and the other residents knew North American doctors made a lot of money and his reaction was amazed shock. "*Ist Wahr?*" he asked. "Is it true?" His behaviour towards me improved slightly after that, but needless to say, I didn't have any social contact with him.

While I worked hard at the hospital, I was only on call every fourth night and every fourth weekend. Compared to the hours I'd been working on the Sunshine Coast, this was almost a vacation, and Bonnie and I took full advantage of this free time to get to know the surrounding countryside. We were helped by Professor Gelbke who seemed to know everything that was going on in his country. He would say, "Oh, there's a *schaefertanz* going on in Rothenburg. You should go there this weekend. Leave early on Friday so you'll have more time and don't bother coming back till Monday morning."

When we weren't attending festivals, visiting vineyards, taking boat trips along the Rhine or exploring museums, castles or cathedrals, we would take the kids to the riverbank parks to play. A family living on the lower floor of our house had several children and our girls played with them so much that they quickly learned the local dialect and Carla, who was an early talker, could soon name all the common colours in both German and English. Then one day several of the doctors at the hospital said to me, "We know where you live, but we would suggest that you *not* live there. You have two beautiful blond kids and they could disappear and you'll never in your life find them again. The gypsies will kidnap them and hide them and they'll be gone."

On her frequent walks with the girls, Bonnie had often walked past the gypsies' riverside encampment and seen kids running around and families with expensive cars that were pulling very nice trailers. She never felt she was in any danger, but after my talk with the other doctors, we decided that an apartment in the village proper might be better for us, though this was partly because living on the outskirts made it hard for Bonnie to get around. She spoke only the basic German she'd managed to learn since our arrival, and she didn't drive, which meant we had to do all of our grocery shopping together, and this was getting a bit awkward. So in mid-September we moved to a place that was within walking distance of the shops and transportation system. We also found a German babysitter, a dear lady who would frequently come and get the kids even when we weren't hiring her to babysit them and take them to the graveyard where her husband was buried. Later we'd ask the kids, "Where were you today?"

They would answer, "Oh, we went to the *friedhof* and we talked to Herr Bohmer!"

Living within the village also meant that Karin could be enrolled in a kindergarten class run by Lutheran sisters. The starting age was three, but the following spring when two-and-a-half-year-old Carla expressed an interest in attending, the sisters asked, "Is she toilet trained?"

"Yes," Bonnie answered.

"Oh, then she can stay."

With all of the advanced procedures I was learning at the hospital and our weekend explorations, the year in Germany passed swiftly, and before we knew it June and our departure was fast approaching. In the final few weeks my chief resident suggested that I complete an income tax rebate form before I left in order to collect the numerous state, church, social security and other taxes I'd been paying during the year.

"I'll help you with it," he said, "because the language is pretty technical."

So in our spare time we worked on filling out all of the forms, finishing them on the day before we were to leave. "What do I do now?" I asked. "Do I send them in?"

"Oh, no," he said. "On your way out of town you're going right by the Income Tax Office. Just go in there and drop them off."

The next morning while Bonnie waited in the car with the children, I ran into the Income Tax Office with the forms and was directed to a waiting area. I joined several people in a line, and when I finally reached the counter, I handed the clerk my papers, anticipating that as soon as I explained what they were for, I would be free to leave and rejoin my waiting family.

"This is my income tax for the year," I told the man. "I'm going back to Canada and I need to leave this with you so that you can send me my rebate."

He looked at the form, checked a few of the numbers and then opened a drawer and asked, "Are hundred mark bills okay with you?"

When I nodded, he pulled out sixteen of these bills, counted them out and handed me the exact amount of my rebate.

"Just like that?" I asked, unable to suppress my astonishment.

"Well, why would I send it to you," he asked, "when I can give it to you right now?"

I was still shaking my head as I walked away, marvelling at the contrast between all the forms and permissions I had needed to work and rent a home, and this incredibly efficient method of issuing a tax refund.

Our homeward journey took Bonnie and I to Denmark, then Holland, and we eventually boarded a cruise ship bound for Calais, France. From there we took a ferry to Dover and both of us felt we were almost home when the famous white cliffs came into view. After visiting London and the Cotswolds we reached Liverpool and boarded a ship that took us to Montreal.

It had been a year of discoveries for all of us, but now we were looking forward to resuming our lives on the Sunshine Coast. In our absence the BC Minister of Health and Hospital Insurance had announced approval for the new hospital in Sechelt, and our friends had written to tell us that construction was well underway. I was eager to get home and see how far this project had progressed.

CHAPTER 5

Not Just Another Hospital

Overjoyed by the prospect of no more long drives to Garden Bay in the middle of the night as well as by the promise of a modern, fully equipped emergency department and operating room, I went back to work on the building committee with new enthusiasm. I was understandably most concerned about the surgical facilities, but I was also a keen member of the grounds committee, and since we would be living with the building for a very long time, I believed it was important to create surroundings that looked good. There were many last-minute details to work out, too, with staffing and in the organization of personnel.

At the same time I was getting back to my routine as a GP/surgeon, dealing with office visits, house calls and on-call duties. By this time Walter Burtnick and Al Swan had each completed a year of surgery, and the other doctors in our practice had done a certain amount as well. They continued to do many procedures on their own, but I was unofficially the lead surgeon and able to share with them the surgical knowledge I'd gained in Germany.

(To my chagrin, I discovered that while I was a very capable and patient instructor in the operating room, I didn't do so well when it came to teaching Bonnie how to drive. After one particularly tense lesson, I escaped into the garden with my clippers and redesigned several shrubs before I calmed down. Fortunately, my brother Verner came to visit and after one lesson with him she mastered the art of driving.)

At the Sechelt clinic I was gradually brought up to date on the condition of my former patients, including an elderly woman who had been a true hypochondriac in every sense of the word. I dreaded having her come into the office because she was such a horrific complainer. Her husband was a long-suffering man who had patiently gone along with her many imagined ailments, and it was he who came into my office shortly after my return. After dealing with his issues, I casually asked him how his wife was doing.

"Oh, she died," he said matter-of-factly.

"She died?" I asked in amazement. "What happened?"

"Oh, I don't know," he said, "but it wasn't anything very much."

Clearly, for him, the cause of her death was just another name in the long list of life-threatening illnesses from which she had imagined herself to be suffering.

Another patient who returned to me was an eighty-year-old woman from Gibsons. She was a big-bosomed lady who was chronically depressed, and as was our practice in those days, I gave her a shot of the hormone Climacteron—probably the best antidepressant ever invented—and told her that it was a vitamin. A couple of months later she returned to the clinic, grinning from ear to ear, and after declaring that she was feeling much better, pulled out her voluminous breasts and began massaging them. Lo and behold, milk came out!

"It's a miracle, Doctor!" she exclaimed. "I'm pregnant!"

It took me a while to convince her that she wasn't going to have a baby, and although I never did reveal the true nature of the injection I'd given her, I'm sure she suspected that it wasn't vitamins.

Logging accidents were still a frequent occurrence on the coast, and so were the flights we had to make up and down the inlets to treat injuries that were too severe for the accident victims to be moved. One day after receiving a call from one of the logging camps located at the head of Narrows Inlet, I boarded a plane piloted by Al Campbell, the helpful airline owner who had told us to bill our camp flights to the logging companies. Starting at the Tyee dock on Porpoise Bay at the head of Sechelt Inlet, our flight was to take us northward, past the entrance to Salmon Inlet, then eastward along Narrows Inlet, a fifteen-kilometre waterway that is bordered on both sides and at the eastern end by high mountains, some rising over fifteen hundred metres above the water. About a third of the way up the inlet, in a section called Tzoonie Narrows, the inlet shrinks to less than fifty metres in width.

Our plane was an old Norseman, one of a line of hardy bush planes designed in 1933 and used as small troop carriers during World War II. As we entered Tzoonie Narrows, Al was flying low to the water and everything was going as it should, but as soon as we got through that passage, we were hit by a fierce windstorm and the plane was forced down onto the absolutely wild water where we were buffeted by wind and waves. As we stared at the eight-foot-high spray walking straight at us, Al radioed the office to tell them what was happening, but the communication was not very good. Getting a little worried, I asked him to let the plane be blown ashore so that we could get off.

"Can't afford to do that, Eric," he said. "I've got a $2,000 deductible on this plane."

Gripping my seat, I stared out at the water flying all around us. "I'll write you a cheque for the deductible right here," I declared. "Just get me ashore!"

He shook his head and we continued to sit there until

suddenly the wind lifted the plane up, and when it came down again, it was tilted to my side with the wing in the water.

"Get out!" Al hollered.

Since his side was up in the air, we climbed out his door and crawled out onto the wing where our combined weight righted the plane again, although we could see that the wing fabric on the passenger side had been torn in the process. We were in a lot of trouble now, and I think Al was about to let the plane go ashore when a boat appeared from the logging camp. They had been monitoring our phone calls and had brought their largest boat out to rescue us. I climbed eagerly aboard it, but Al elected to stay with his plane, eventually riding out the storm and taxiing the aircraft to the nearest logging camp.

Meanwhile, I was taken to the injured man, a schizophrenic who had faked the severity of his injury and really did not need my help.

Most surgeons have their areas of special interest, and mine was trauma, partly because the patient's condition was none of my doing. In later years with the advent of enforced speed limits, the use of seatbelts and crackdowns on drinking drivers, trauma on the Sunshine Coast took a noticeable dip. When I first came here, however, there were frequent emergencies of this kind, and as the lead surgeon in an isolated community, I had free rein to treat each injury as I saw fit, often employing some very unorthodox measures.

One such case was a logging accident I attended in the mountains east of Clowhom Lake, which is located at the head of Salmon Inlet. I received a radio phone call to come up there because a faller had a badly damaged leg and they were afraid to move him. Apparently he had slipped and tumbled backwards, bringing the running chainsaw down onto his leg. The logging company dispatched a helicopter to pick up Al Swan and myself, but when we reached the accident site the pilot told us there was no place for him to land. Consequently, while

Al stayed with the helicopter, I got off on the beach and walked three miles up the hill, partly along a crude roadway that was under construction and partly over a slash of newly fallen trees, to the site where the injured man and his partner were located.

Wes Anderson, the faller, had landed in a small ravine and it took only a moment for me to realize that he had sawn completely through both bones of his lower right leg in the mid-calf area. Fortunately, he'd had the foresight to wrap his belt around his thigh and wind it tight enough to effectively staunch the flow of blood. He had also put the nearly sawed-off leg against the far bank of the ravine and then rammed the proximal part into it. The first thing he asked for when I arrived was something for the pain. Obligingly, I established an intra-venous line into his arm and injected some morphine into the line. To my horror, he stopped breathing, and I found myself in a most awkward situation, crouched down in this gully with no idea of what to do. Then I looked up at his partner, who was standing on the bank above us.

"Jump on the leg!" I ordered.

The man gaped at me.

"Jump on it!" I ordered again, with such vehemence that he obeyed, jumping onto the leg and knocking it totally askew. The shock caused my patient to take a deep breath and he was revived. After that I was not about to give him any more morphine.

"You'll just have to tough it out," I said.

Meanwhile, the pilot had managed to land the helicopter on a spot below us where the roadway cut into a steep bank. He set the plane down crossways with its nose snubbed against the cliff and its tail sticking out over a sheer drop-off. Al got out and hurried up the hill, and by the time he reached us, the patient's vital signs had stabilized enough for us to splint the leg. With the help of Al, the logger's partner and the co-pilot, we were able to carry our patient on a stretcher down to the helicopter, but then we faced the problem of lifting off from our precarious position on the cliff. Since going straight up or forward was impossible, the pilot flipped the helicopter over in an upside-down manoeuvre that set my heart pounding louder than the rotor blades. Just when I was sure we were all going to die, he righted the helicopter and we were on our way.

Although the patient survived, his leg was so badly injured that a year later it had to be amputated below the knee. Eventually, though, he did return to falling. Vic Walters, who owned the logging company, was so grateful for our efforts that he presented us with a set of hand-held walkie-talkies in case we ever ran into a similar situation in the future.

This accident was just one more reminder of the constant danger that West Coast loggers faced, and the grim consequences that could result from even the slightest mistake. Too many times my only role was to pronounce the victim dead at the scene or to examine the body on the autopsy table. This occurred with a young logger who had taken an unscheduled break from his duties to smoke a marijuana cigarette. To escape detection, he knelt behind the back end of a yarder—the huge machine that brings logs from where they've been felled to a landing where they can be loaded onto trucks. This machine is mounted on a track so that it can move back and forth as needed to access all of the timber in a certain area. On this occasion, not expecting anyone to be behind his machine, the operator shifted into reverse and the yarder moved backwards, running over the young man and killing him instantly. Later the Worker's Compensation Board tried to force the logging company to pay the costs relating to the accident, claiming that the man had not been warned about the dangers of standing behind the loader. They were unsuccessful, however, because the company owners could prove that they had been very diligent in their safety procedures and had provided adequate warnings about the dangers of working around heavy-duty equipment. They also had a fully equipped ambulance and gave first aid training to their employees.

Many fatalities occurred when loggers were hit by logs during the yarding process. Like giant baseball bats, the logs will swing from the yarder's boom in sometimes unpredictable directions, catching unwary victims by surprise. There also continued to be deaths from drowning, and one of these had an ironic twist. A big, strong young man had fallen off a barge and drowned. Two hours later as I viewed his body, I saw that the front of his t-shirt read, "Life's a bitch—and then you die!" Another drowning was the result of a suicide by a man suffering from a mental disorder. Early one morning he drove his truck at a high speed down School Road, onto the public wharf and into the water. To ensure that he did not change his mind at the last minute, he had handcuffed himself to the steering wheel.

One grisly death yielded a surprise that was not readily apparent. The police had been called to the Trail Bay beach in Sechelt where a wooden box had been washed ashore. Inside were a pair of lower legs, disarticulated at the knees. The legs were burnt, the toenails had been removed and I found remnants of burned socks. Since I had no facilities or resources for diagnosing either the cause of death or the victim, I sent the legs to Vancouver where a forensic examination determined that they were bear legs. A jokester had the biggest laugh.

In early November 1964 we began final preparations for moving patients from Garden Bay to the new hospital in Sechelt. Already the furnishings and equipment were in place, shelves were being stocked with supplies, schedules were being worked out and staffing arrangements finalized. Unfortunately, many of the people with whom we had worked so closely over the years would not be joining us in the new facility. They included our administrator, Bill Milligan, who had resigned his post in June, shortly after my return from Germany. In his place, Norman Buckley was working hard to make the transition between the old and new as smooth as possible. Gerry Jervis left us at this time as well, retiring to Sechelt with her partner,

The new hospital in Sechelt opened in November 1964, a modern building with all the equipment we needed to perform most of the diagnostic and surgical procedures we'd been sending our patients off the coast to receive.

Margaret McIntyre, (author of *Place of Quiet Waters*, a book about their adventures building a cabin on Nelson Island).

The loss of these staff members was offset by the anticipation we all felt over working in a modern building with twenty-five acute-care beds and all the equipment we needed to perform the diagnostic and surgical procedures that we'd been sending our patients off the coast to receive. We even had our own radiologist living on the coast, and an internist who would commute to our hospital from Vancouver.

The official opening date was set for November 29, but as with anything connected with the medical profession, nature dictated a different time schedule. Late in the afternoon of the day before the move a young girl came into my office with abdominal pain, which I quickly diagnosed as acute appendicitis. Since much of our staff and operating room equipment had already been moved to Sechelt, we quickly mobilized an operating team, transported my patient to the new hospital and carried out a successful appendectomy.

That evening while the medical staff and various dignitaries attended a celebratory banquet at the Sechelt Inn's Green Thumb Room, our O.R. supervisor, Jean Stewart, was left alone in the huge, empty, and somewhat spooky new hospital to care for the patient as she recovered from her surgery. Meanwhile, Bonnie and I were enjoying ourselves at the celebration, and I drank a toast to the fact that I had made my last long drive to Garden Bay. We had just been served our dessert and coffee when one of the hotel staff advised me that I had a phone call. The nurse at Garden Bay was calling to say that a woman had been admitted who was about to give birth. Suppressing a groan, I left the party and drove to Garden Bay where I delivered a healthy baby girl. By then it was well past midnight and I decided to spend the rest of the night at the hospital. In the morning I installed the new mother and her baby in my car and we joined the caravan transporting patients to Sechelt. To this day, I don't let the mother, Melanie Joe, forget how she ruined that night for me.

That afternoon the Honorable Eric Martin, then Minister of Health and Hospital Insurance, cut the ceremonial ribbon and

This is Melanie Joe, the lady who wrecked the celebratory party for me with the last delivery in Garden Bay.

the new St. Mary's Hospital was born.

With the closure of the Garden Bay hospital, we moved our Pender Harbour clinic to a renovated house in nearby Madeira Park. The waiting room in this clinic had once been a living room and it was so huge that the local people began using it as a gathering place. It would be full when I arrived at eleven o'clock and I would think, *My God! I'm not even late and they're all here!* When the first patient came in to see me, I'd say, "Gee, I'm sorry I'm so late."

"Oh no, no, Doc," the patient would respond, "you're right on time. I just came early so I could visit with my friend. He's seeing you next."

After consulting with me, the patients would return to the waiting room, spot another acquaintance or two and visit with them. Our receptionist, Lewella Duncan, who knew them all, would serve refreshments, so it was like a big coffee klatch.

Operating room supervisor Jean Stewart had a gentle yet effective touch, and was a great one to create skits.

The population at the south end of the Sunshine Coast was much larger than at the north end, and many of our patients from the north end were willing to come to our Sechelt clinic. So when Walter Burtnick moved to Sechelt, we decided to man the Madiera Park clinic for only two days a week. They were big clinics, however, running from eleven in the morning until late in the day and often included house calls.

In Sechelt, house calls were now reduced in number, and most of them cost me little more than lost sleep or a disrupted schedule. There were a few, however, that could have exacted a much higher price. One of these occurred when I was called some time after midnight to visit a house that was located on the Trail Bay waterfront. The family feared that one of their relatives had broken his neck, and while I doubted this was so, I could not risk ignoring the request. As I drove into Sechelt, I spotted two of the local Mounties—Bob Selwood and Bill Destree—in their car parked at one of the garages, and since they were both friends of mine, I pulled in to have a quick word with them. When I left, I told them where I was going and said jokingly, "If you don't see me drive past here again in fifteen minutes, come looking for me."

My patient was in the living room, lying on a dilapidated old sofa. On the back of the couch lay a large pile of dirty old clothes. As I expected, the man was very drunk and a quick examination revealed that he did not have a broken neck.

"There's nothing wrong with him," I told the family. I closed my doctor's bag and had just got to my feet when the pile of dirty clothes moved. That's when I realized there was a man inside them, and the next thing I knew, he was weaving towards me with a twelve-inch butcher knife in his hands! Keeping the couch between him and myself, and holding my bag in front of me as a shield, we circled around the passed-out patient. The man had a glazed, dumb look in his eyes, and I just knew he would use the knife if I gave him an opening. I was getting close to panicking when suddenly the door exploded inward and my two Mountie friends appeared. They grabbed the man from behind and unceremoniously dragged him outside.

"If you've had enough in there, you're welcome to join us, Doc," Bob called back to me.

Later, after the man had been safely locked behind bars, Bob and Bill explained that to pass the time they had driven by the house to see how I was doing. I hate to think what the outcome might have been if they hadn't done so!

Another unusual visit involved Jennie, a lovely, elderly lady who lived near the intersection of Lockyer Road and Highway 101. One dark, rainy November night she called to say that there was a sick man at her house, and since she had no vehicle she could not bring him to the hospital. She met me at the door and promptly led me through the kitchen, the living room and finally into her bedroom where she easily pushed her bed aside to reveal a trap door.

"Leads to the root cellar," she said, and opening the trap door, she shone her flashlight into the dark interior, lighting the face of the craziest-looking, white-haired, white-bearded man that I had ever seen. He had the wildest eyes and kept smacking his lips, almost like he was drooling.

Jennie turned to me and said calmly, "There he is."

"I'm not going down in that hole!" I exclaimed and quickly closed the trap door.

She grinned. "You're schmart, Doctor." She went on to explain that while she was sitting at the table eating her supper, this man had appeared at her door. She had let him in and then, realizing that he was crazy, had managed to entice him into the root cellar. Once he was safely locked away, she telephoned me.

The only thing for me to do was to call the police who arrived a short time later and took the man away in a straitjacket. No one seemed to know who he was, although he fit the profile of a legendary Roberts Creek character known as Belgian Joe, a hermit who had apparently hung around Roberts Creek for a while near the start of World War II, then disappeared into the hills and was not seen again. He was rumoured to have been living up Mt. Elphinstone and it's possible that he had drifted down to Lockyer Road and landed at the woman's house. In any event, the man was taken to an asylum in Vancouver and died some time later without ever being officially identified.

Not all of the situations I encountered, however, were from house calls. One fall weekend I took my boat up to Deserted Bay to visit with Pete Jackson at his logging camp and do some hunting. Minnie Solberg and her partner, Henry Dray, were living there as squatters and acted as caretakers of the camp whenever it was shut down. Although their somewhat primitive house had no running water, Henry had built a huge waterwheel, which produced electricity for them, and he had rigged up an antennae so that they could watch television. Normally the couple got along reasonably well, but on this day

Minnie was acting a bit erratic, and Henry claimed that she had beaten him up that morning. Totally fed up with her, he had radioed the police, and I happened to be there when the Mounties arrived.

"Henry says you beat him with a two-by-four," one of the officers said to Minnie.

She shook her head. "Did not," she said firmly.

Henry, who was standing with us, shouted, "You did, too!"

"Did not!"

"Did, too!"

This exchange continued for several minutes. Finally the police officer turned to Minnie and asked, "Well, what *did* you do?"

"I hit him with a two-by-*six*!" she declared.

At this point everyone cracked up, including Henry.

"Oh, forget it," he said. "I'm not charging her."

One patient whose appearance always put us on guard was Charlie, a hulking old logger from Madeira Park. According to local legend, in his youth he had been involved in a fight with a Sechelt chief, who was another big man, and the two had stood toe to toe and slugged it out for the best part of an hour before they both collapsed in a heap. At any rate, Charlie was subject to bouts of insanity, when he was rumoured to bay at the full moon and fire his rifle at it. Once he boarded a southbound bus, brandishing a shotgun and vowing to straighten out those bandits in Victoria once and for all. Al Swan had him committed to Riverview but, with their usual ineptness, the staff there returned him home within a week. A few days later Charlie came into the clinic and was as pleasant as could be.

"Alan," he asked with a big smile, "did you send me to Riverview?"

The man was acting so friendly that Al thought the situation was diffused, and he answered honestly, "Yes, I did."

The patient's grin instantly turned into a mean one, and he

said, "Alan, I can understand that you thought you had to do it, but if you ever commit me again, I will kill you!"

Needless to say, Al never committed him again and neither did I.

In addition to his occasional bouts of psychosis, Charlie suffered from terrible varicose veins and varicose ulcers that required both legs to be bandaged. He would visit our Madeira clinic in the middle of the afternoon when we were absolutely run off our feet, and when his turn came, he would shuffle into the office as though he had all the time in the world and would slowly remove the bandages, which had not been changed since his last visit. It would take about forty-five minutes before he had the bandages off and we could redress them. He stunk to high heaven and the whole office became almost unusable for the rest of the day, but we could not rush him because we were all scared that he would turn mean. Eventually the local Mounties and a judge committed Charlie back to Riverview where he was diagnosed with bipolar disorder and given medication that allowed him to live out his remaining years peaceably in the home of his daughter.

Although we dealt with many tragedies in our practice, we did have some gratifying outcomes, such as one that followed an accident at Chatterbox Falls. This forty-metre (120-foot) waterfall at the head of Princess Louisa Inlet has been the site of many fatal accidents, partly because visitors ignore the signs warning them not to go beyond the protective rope that runs along the trail above the falls. While it is tempting to view the cascade from the edge of the cliff, the moss clinging to the rocks is so slippery that it is easy to lose your footing. One day in 1966, a sixteen-year-old naval cadet from Tacoma was hiking up to the falls with a group of fellow Sea Scouts when he accidentally slipped into the river and was swept over the falls. Fortunately he survived the plunge and managed to drag himself onto a rock where rescuers were able to reach him. He was brought to the hospital in Sechelt, and we successfully repaired his shattered knee and other injuries. Shortly after he returned home his mother wrote to thank us for doing what her Seattle doctors said was a good job on her son's leg. About ten years later I received another message inviting me to come to the boy's graduation from medical school. Apparently I had inspired him to become a doctor![24]

Then their was a near-drowning. It occurred just at dusk near the end of October when two fishing buddies—Jack Nelson and a local RCMP officer, Orv Underhill—were returning home from Kunechin Point in Sechelt Inlet. A sudden squall came up and their boat capsized, leaving them clinging to the hull, and as the cold and dark settled over them, their situation seemed hopeless. A true ectomorph, Orv lost body heat quickly and became incoherent, but the other man, Jack Nelson, was stouter so he was able to function much longer. Fortunately, shortly after the accident, beachcomber Jack Goosen, returning from an expedition around Storm Bay, swept his spotlight in front of him and thought he saw something flash over to his left. Curious, he turned the spotlight on the area for a longer look and discovered the two men.

By the time they reached the hospital, Jack Nelson was in stable condition, but Orv was seriously hypothermic, with a cardiac arrhythmia (irregularity). We started him at once on a regimen of warm intravenous fluids, warm saline gavages and warm enemas.

He survived.

Often with accidents the need for immediate action means that diagnosis and treatment decisions don't always receive the careful deliberation that might be given if time was on the side of the physician and surgeon. When the emergency is over, however, it is easy to look back and wonder if the choice made was the best possible treatment under the circumstances. This occurred one day when two young motorcyclists from Vancouver were hit by a truck. Both patients had mangled left legs that needed to be amputated in order to save their lives. After recovering from their surgeries, they returned to Vancouver, but both harboured doubts about their treatment, and a year later I received a letter from their lawyer questioning the necessity for the amputations. Clearly he was under the impression that this country doctor had over-reacted. Fortunately, I had taken detailed photographs of the injured legs and was able to send copies to the lawyer. Soon after he reviewed them, the case was dropped. (Later the couple were married.)

Both Pender Harbour and Roberts Creek were home to colonies of hippies during these years, although they only came to us "regular doctors" when all else had failed. There was no point in sending them a bill for our services because, even if they had an address, they simply wouldn't pay. Sometimes they would offer to chop wood for us but they never did. Usually their babies were delivered at home, and afterwards they immediately went into celebratory mode. On one of these occasions after the drugs and booze wore off some hours later, they realized they hadn't delivered the placenta and the mother had lost a great deal of blood. They brought her to the hospital then and while I was dealing with the placenta, one of the nurses tried unsuccessfully to find a vein to start an IV. Finally in exasperation, the patient said, "Oh, give it to my friend there. He can do it." And he did. In fact, most of the hippies on the Coast could find a vein very easily. On the few occasions when they did come to the hospital for a delivery, some tried to eat their placentas—raw. It was difficult to watch.

The police were always involved in accident cases, and consequently we developed a close association with our local RCMP officers, including a particularly aggressive sergeant who seemed to be trying to personally eradicate all of the marijuana in the world. While visiting him in his office one evening for reasons related to a coroner's case, he took me into a back room and proudly revealed his most recent accomplishment.

Nailed to a four-foot-by-eight-foot sheet of plywood hung several dozen upside-down plants.

"Marijuana plants," he said proudly. "I found them in a
clearing behind Elphinstone High School." He was obviously
delighted with this opportunity to teach the high school kids a
lesson, but at that very moment a most irate elderly gentleman
stomped into the office. Wiljo Wiren lived behind the school,
and he declared angrily that some rowdy students had pulled
out all of his tomato plants. There was a deafening silence in
the room while the Mountie fought to regain his composure.
Then, without looking at me, he explained to Wiljo that he
would pursue the issue with due diligence. I must confess that
in my inexperienced opinion, the upside-down tomato plants
hanging in the back room like dead turkeys certainly could
have passed for marijuana plants!

A more serious incident occurred several years later when
Dr. John Farrer called me into the Emergency Room to see a
female patient who had been stabbed in the chest by her husband. She was failing very fast, and all we could do was to
open her chest to see if we could deal with the major damage.
However, by then her chest cavity was already totally full of
blood and she died before we could repair her wounds. The
following day Dan Devlin, the coroner, asked me to do the
autopsy.

"I can't," I said. "I did some surgery on her."

But there was no one else available, and finally I allowed
Dan to convince me that this was just a routine case and my
dual role would not amount to anything. Lo and behold, it
ended up as a major criminal case that was tried before the BC
Supreme Court with Justice Tom Berger presiding. When they
called for the doctor who had dealt with the case, I took the
stand where I was duly cross-examined and then dismissed. I
had just returned to my seat when they called for the next witness—the pathologist who had done the autopsy. Once again,
I took the stand and I must say this caused quite a stir in the

courtroom because it was most unorthodox to have the same person be the expert witness on both sides of a case. I held my breath, awaiting for repercussions from the bench, but after a moment Justice Berger turned back to the counsellors and nodded for them to continue. The case proceeded and the woman's husband was sentenced to jail.

Of course, most of our surgeries were not emergencies and many of them were routine enough that we could afford to joke with one another in the operating room. However, one pretty operating room nurse, Pat, was so painfully shy that she reminded me of a frightened deer, and she took everything so seriously that I tried not to kid her—although sometimes I couldn't help myself. One morning we were operating on a man with a dirty bum that had little stool balls stuck to the hairs around the rectum.

"Will-knots," I remarked as the young nurse worked to remove them. When she looked at me in confusion, I said, "No matter how hard you pull, they simply 'will not' come off!"

Uncharacteristically, Pat exploded with laughter, and it took a few moments before she was able to get back to the task at hand. Later she explained that her husband was an RCMP officer, and as a young recruit at the Regina training campus, one of his jobs was to clean "will-knots" off the Musical Ride horses.

Humorous moments weren't limited to the operating room. A seventy-year-old patient from Roberts Creek had told me that she used to live in a small mining town on the northern BC coast. Knowing that Wally Vosburgh, our part-time radiologist, had practised in that town when he was a young GP, I found it strange that when he and my patient met at the hospital, neither acknowledged that fact. I casually mentioned this to my patient one day and she revealed that she had been a madam at one of the town's brothels, and our radiologist's job included examining the girls every three months for possible venereal disease. Then the woman told me she was having a problem with her "foo-foo valve." Not understanding what this was, I looked at her questioningly and she pointed to her labia. I snorted out a short laugh, and she roared with laughter at my discomfiture.

Mild practical jokes were another source of amusement at our clinic and it was always easy to play one on Al Swan, partly because he was very predictable. Every morning, for instance, he would check his daybook to make sure he wasn't double-booked for anything. Once while he was doing this, he saw the name of a particularly difficult patient. This lady was an endless talker and always took an extraordinary amount of Al's time with each visit. I happened to be passing the office just then and heard him tell our receptionist, Betty, "Give me fifteen minutes with this patient and then come in and say that I'm needed for an emergency at the hospital."

Betty agreed and we all went on with our day. At the appointed time I saw the patient head for Al's office, and after

My toast at Cita and Kjeld's wedding was translated into Tagalog and drew gales of laughter from the guests. To this day, I am convinced that Blanca doctored my speech by inserting some risqué elements.

a while I heard Betty make her announcement. I waited five seconds for her to return to the reception area then went to Al's office and opened the door.

"Al," I said, keeping my face straight, "I've got to go to the hospital anyway. I'll look after your emergency." Then I quickly closed the door on his protests.

In the end he accepted the joke graciously.

Although it wasn't meant as a prank, Al's wife Rosa un-intentionally caused a situation that was amusing to everyone except Al. One of his trademarks when I first met him was a Harris tweed jacket, which he wore every day for about seven months of each year. No matter how many other jackets Rosa bought for him, he wouldn't part with the tweed. Then early one fall Archie, a ne'er-do-well patient, came into his office wearing the Harris tweed, which Rosa had donated to the thrift shop. She hadn't got around to telling Al what she'd done, but he recognized his jacket at once and spent the whole visit upset and frustrated, wondering how he could get it back!

Occasionally other staff members were the ones to pull the pranks. I'm sure this happened at the wedding of Cita Bacris and Kjeld Hanson. As part of a journey to see and work in various parts of Canada, five Filipina nurses came to work at St. Mary's. They lived in the nurses' residence on the property, and once in a while entertained us by performing dances in historic costumes that were traditional to the Philippines. It wasn't long before three of them, Lena Filler (Beyser), Blanca Reyes (Bunbury) and Cita were snapped up by available bachelors. When I was asked to give a toast to the bride at Cita's wedding, I asked Blanca to translate my speech into Tagalog, using phonetics to help me say the words correctly. It was a reasonably funny toast, but not funny enough to warrant the gales of laughter it drew from the Filipino guests. To this day, I am convinced that Blanca doctored my speech by inserting some risqué stories of their past!

Although an animal hospital had opened in Gibsons in 1963, we still occasionally complied with requests to treat animals when the veterinarian was either not available or too far away. Such was the case when a well-off local businessman asked if I would look at one of his sheep that was short of breath. After an examination I gave the animal shots for both pneumonia and heart failure and then hoped for the best. As I was packing up my bag, the man suggested that I submit a bill on his Medical Services Insurance number.

"No," I said, "I'd rather do it for free than cheat."

Red-faced, he hastily pulled several bills from his wallet and thrust them into my hands, all the while stumbling over apologies for making such a request.

A somewhat similar incident occurred after a wealthy Vancouver lady brought her little dog into the Emergency Room. Her pet was convulsing and she was frantic, and at first Al Swan and I were at a loss to determine the cause of the convulsions. After concluding that the dog, a lactating bitch, might be suffering from a calcium deficiency, we gave her an intravenous shot of calcium and the animal's condition quickly normalized. The woman returned to Vancouver where she wrote us to say that, according to her vet, we had saved the dog's life, and we could expect a token of her gratitude. Since the woman's husband owned a popular men's clothing store, Al and I were envisioning argyle sweaters and fine silk ties. A few days later we received a package from the store. Inside was a large bottle of Old Spice after-shave lotion, clearly marked as a "Sample—not to be sold."

Just four years after it opened, the new hospital was already proving inadequate for the Sunshine Coast's growing population. The average occupancy in 1964 was 4,926 patient days. By 1968 it was 13,464 patient days or 105 percent of capacity, and we were now doing almost 1,800 surgeries a year.[25] Consequently, we began making plans for expanding the facility to include a second storey with thirteen acute care beds and twenty-two extended care beds, as well as an enlarged emergency room on the main floor and the completion of a physiotherapy department in the basement. This expansion was approved in a February 1969 referendum.[26]

A month earlier my friend Wally Vosburgh, who was our radiologist, had advised me to complete my surgical training. "You can do all of your surgeries now as a GP," he said, "but the time will come in BC when they might not let you do so." I knew he was right, and since I was due for a second sabbatical, I began searching for another surgical residency, applying first to the Vancouver General Hospital where I was interviewed by a pompous bureaucrat.

"Well," he said at the end of the interview, "we can give you a residency here at VGH, but you will have to start all over again at year one."

"But I've already completed two years," I spluttered.

"Yes, but they were undertaken somewhere else, so we can't accept them."

Furious with his attitude, I walked away with absolutely no intention of repeating my previous training, especially not after the phenomenal surgical experience I had acquired in Germany. Instead I applied to the Mercy Hospital in San Diego where I had done my first year of surgical residency. Sister Alexi, who was in charge of surgery, was delighted to hear from me. "But unfortunately," she said, "we're no longer in control of our residency program. It's now being run by the University of California, San Diego branch." She gave me the name of the professor in charge of the program, who advised me that there was no room for anyone to step into a third-year spot. Meanwhile, Al Swan, who had spent two of his sabbaticals as a surgical resident at the The Queen's Medical Center in Honolulu, contacted the surgical department there and recommended me for their program. His promotion on my behalf was so effective that the director said they would make a spot for me, but just before I accepted this position, I received another call from Sister Alexi. "I've heard about an opening at the Kaiser Foundation Hospital in San Francisco," she said. "They're looking for a third-year resident to fill a vacancy in their program." Since San Francisco appealed to me more than Hawaii, I immediately phoned the chief of surgery who invited me to come down for an interview.

When I told Wally Vosburgh what I was doing, he said, "Eric, your hair is too long. You can't go there looking that scruffy." Following his advice once again, I had my barber, George Flay, give me a brush cut.

A few days later I arrived at the Kaiser Hospital, which took up one corner of a huge, sprawling medical campus that was considered the best health care model in the United States. The chief of surgery, Peter Dunlop Smith, known as PD, was a short, grey-haired man with a gentle lop-sided smile. He was dyslexic, and although he could certainly read and operate, he couldn't write properly, and he was not a gifted speaker. I was thirty-five at this time, and with all of my experience, I was feeling pretty confident as I answered his questions. However, there were awkward pauses in the conversation and after one of these he said abruptly, "Well, do you want the job?"

"Yes!" I said, taken by surprise.

"Okay, you've got it."

"Just like that?" I asked.

"Yeah." Then he stood and said, "Let's go down to the cafeteria for lunch. I want you to meet a few people."

As we walked into the cafeteria, jammed with hospital staff, I looked around and realized that all of the men had hair down to their shoulders and faces full of hair. Trying to appear nonchalant, I took my place in the line-up for service, but I soon realized that people were looking at me with more than a little curiosity. Some of my colleagues told me later that the stares were because everyone thought I must be a marine. (Of course, it didn't take me long to let my brush cut grow out and by the end of the year I had hair as long as the rest as well as a beard and mustache!)

I knew by the end of lunch that I wanted to take the job that PD offered, but the position required someone to stay for two years, one as a resident and the next as a chief resident. Before I could agree to that or anything else, I needed to talk with both Bonnie and Al Swan. I called Bonnie first, and as always, she put aside whatever misgivings she may have had and told me to go for it. Then I called Al. "This is the situation," I told him, "either I stay two years or I don't get the job."

His response was prompt. "Stay," he said. "We'll make it happen."

Over the next few days I completed the arrangements needed to start the residency program and then returned to Sechelt to prepare my practice and my family for our move to San Francisco in July.

CHAPTER **6**

Golden Gate Immersion

Our family had grown since our first sabbatical, and we now had four children, Karin, Carla, Guy and two-year-old Mark. This meant that relocating to San Francisco was a little more complicated than our move to Ludwigshafen, but we were fortunate to find a house for rent in a location that was good for my family and within easy commuting distance to the hospital. As usual, Bonnie looked after organizing our new home and making arrangements for Karin, Carla and Guy to attend school, leaving me free to focus on my new job.

P.D. Smith was in charge of the hospital's eight modern operating rooms, but separate chiefs were responsible for the various sub-specialities. Among the staff members were a few Canadian O.R. nurses who made me feel right at home.

My first mentor, and eventually a close friend, was Sean Holman, a refined hippie who loved smoking pot. We met while we were scrubbing for the first case in which I was to assist him—a mastectomy for cancer.

After talking for a few minutes he asked, "Have you ever done this operation before, Doc?"

"Yes, I have," I responded.

"Cool, man! Then you do it," he said and walked away.

Sean was a single dad about ten years older than myself, and he owned a rustic house in Mill Valley as well as a ski chalet. When my residency was over and I was preparing to return to Sechelt, he could not understand why I would want to leave San Francisco. It wasn't until he came to visit us on the Sunshine Coast that he understood.

As in Germany, because of my age and my extensive operating room experience during my previous residencies and on the Sunshine Coast, P.D. gave me unlimited privileges and responsibilities in the surgical department, and it was here that I learned to make judgement calls from yet another mentor, a thoracic surgeon from Iran named Al Shamma, a name that means "candle maker." Chest surgery was rather mysterious to me at that time, but he taught me to approach all operations methodically, employing the same sound, basic principles that I would use in handling any tissue.

"Do this," he said, "and there is virtually no operation that should frighten you."

To put myself in this frame of mind, I developed a favourite quote, which has often been used to characterize me: before embarking on a difficult case, I say, "Here goes. The Lord hates a coward!"

Another surgeon taught me about surgical limitations, such as knowing when *not* to operate. "When the forces of nature are going to make a patient die," he told me, "leave it at that. It is not your duty to have them die on the O.R. table!"

I also learned from my patients. A young man who had become exasperated with his stomach ulcer pain tried to end his discomfort by shooting the spot with a revolver. He was a mess, but I noticed that the bullet had gone right through the ulcer. Needless to say, there were complications during the surgery and I expected a lot of pain post-op, but strangely, he didn't request any pain medicine. I was amazed and when I told him so, he explained that his friends were bringing him pot to smoke, which handled his pain just fine. That was my first exposure to the pain control properties of marijuana. The nurses were cool with this practice and since it seemed that everyone was using it, I let him smoke as much as he wanted.

While much of my attention in San Francisco was focussed on learning, I had a lot of spare time and there were many weekends when I wasn't on call. These became family times, and we used them well for there was much to see and do. In the city we visited Golden Gate Park, which was closed to cars on Sunday and open to bikers and hikers. At other times we explored the Napa Valley, Yosemite Park, Squaw Valley, Tahoe, and of course, Disneyland. Once we drove to Booneville, in the hinterland a hundred and eighty-five kilometres north of the city. This town of barely a thousand people was located in the picturesque Anderson Valley, which was reminiscent of Scottish mountain country and isolated from the outside world by green mountains, steep roads and hairpin turns. Here, some of the people still spoke Boontling, a strange mixture of Scottish Gaelic, Irish, native Pomoan, Spanish and made-up words. The language had been invented in the mid-1800s by a couple of brothers sitting around in the local saloon as a method of communicating that wives and enemies couldn't understand. At one time everyone in the town spoke little else, but by 1969 the language was only being kept alive by a few old-timers and even fewer new conscripts.

Soon after settling into our new home in San Francisco, Bonnie and I became good friends with our neighbours, Ann and Bob Harrington. He was a school principal and descendent of the old San Francisco family that owned Harrington's Saloon, a remnant from the gold rush days and the only original saloon left in the west. The Harrington brothers took turns running the establishment, and since Bob's turn was every Saturday, it became a bi-weekly tradition for Bonnie and me to pick up Ann and drive down to the saloon. While Bob closed up shop, we'd have a Golden Cadillac, a pricey little drink made with Galiano, white crème de cacao and cream. Afterwards, we'd all go to dinner and the theatre.

As a son of San Francisco, Bob knew a lot of good eating places, but I had another way of discovering great dining experiences. Every time I had an ethnic patient, I would ask, "What is your favourite restaurant in San Francisco?" and "Where do you go for ethnic food?" We would go to the place they named and try it out. Another source of information was Charlie Jackson, the chief resident for my first year at Kaiser. He knew his way around the Haight-Ashbury district and often took Bonnie and me there.

After I became a chief resident in 1971, it was my turn to do some mentoring. One of my juniors was an Ebo from Nigeria named Tom Chinema ("son of man"), who married a mail-order bride from his home country, and Bonnie and I were privileged to attend their fascinating wedding. They eventually had two delightful kids, and to help program them to go back to Nigeria, the parents would not allow the children to eat sweets such as candies, chocolate or Coke. After Tom finally finished his training, the family visited us in Sechelt on their way home to Nigeria. It was the last we ever heard of them, and we have always wondered if they were victims of the violence in that country.

Another intern was Barrie Kassen, a doctor from Saskatoon who was planning to go to the D.M. Anderson Hospital in Texas for further training. As we were both Saskatoon guys, he and his wife, Susan, became our really good friends. We had met when he came onto my service for his month's rotation, but we hit it off so well that at the end of that month he traded with another intern so he could stay on for another month. Out of the blue one day he said, "I'd like to join your clinic in Sechelt." I phoned Al Swan and said, "I've got a good guy here who wants to join our practice." Al agreed and the Kassens moved to Sechelt where Barrie worked with us for several years before leaving to finish his residency in internal medicine.

One of my surgeries during our final year in San Francisco was performed on a fifty-year-old man who had infarcted his small intestine; in other words, the intestine was dead. As chief resident I made my own decisions, and in this case I had two clear choices—I could let him die or I could remove the intestine and subject him to a life of intravenous nutrition. I chose to remove the intestine, but during the surgical rounds that followed, it was the common consensus of my fellow surgeons that I had made the wrong decision. Five years later while completing a residency in anatomic pathology at this same hospital, I found myself doing an autopsy on this man. When it was completed, I made a point of contacting his wife and asked her whether those five years had been good or bad for him. She said that they had been good enough and that they had often remembered me with gratitude.

At the end of two years, armed with the required skills and knowledge to pass the examinations to become a fully qualified BC surgeon, I said goodbye to my friends and colleagues at the Kaiser Hospital, and Bonnie, I and the children returned to the Sunshine Coast. There we discovered that during our absence time had not stood still. In Gibsons plans were being made by the CBC for the filming of a new television series called *The Beachcombers*. In Sechelt a huge open-pit gravel mine was being proposed by Construction Aggregates, to be located just northwest of the hospital, with a conveyor belt running from the mine and underneath Highway 101 to Trail Bay in order to transport gravel to sea-going barges. In Pender Harbour the old hospital had been reopened as a hotel, and the community there was working hard to establish an ambulatory service clinic, which would include the full-time services of a general practitioner.

Of course, it took a while for my friends and patients on the Sunshine Coast to get used to the changes in me as well for now, besides sporting long hair, I had a full beard. On our first night back we went to a rather formal local restaurant for supper, and the hostess, Joyce, who had once been a neighbour of ours, said, "I'm sorry, sir, but we don't allow hippies to come in." Then she saw Bonnie and the kids and squealed with laughter. A few days later we went to the annual salmon barbecue put on by the Sechelt Indian Band where I sat down beside a woman I'd known for many years and on whom I had performed at least three operations. When I mentioned the surgeries and asked about the outcomes, her eyes opened wider and wider. After a few minutes I moved on, but as I left I heard her say to her son, "That hippie knows all about me!" Her son laughed as he told her who I was.

I returned from the Kaiser Foundation Hospital in San Francisco to the Sunshine Coast, and we found that in our absence there had been many changes.

Unfortunately, the hospital expansion, which I had expected to see completed on my return, was months behind schedule and St. Mary's was in a shambles. The sink in the emergency ward had yet to be installed, a hole in the wall marked the place for the new sterilizer, and the reception desk was stuck in a corridor in the basement, while the rest of the office desks had been squeezed into the board room.[27] But the new operating unit was perfect. Unbeknownst to me, the planning committee had phoned someone at the Kaiser Foundation Hospital and asked them to describe my favourite operating room so they could design our new one with that in mind. However, before I had a chance to use it, I had to spend a month in Vancouver and Seattle studying and taking exams for my certification as a fully qualified surgeon.

In 1965 Bonnie and I had purchased a seven-acre property in Selma Park and built a house on it. But on our return in the fall of 1971 we decided to build another house, higher up the hill. It was at this time that I also began teaching surgical techniques to medical students who had obtained temporary assignments on the Sunshine Coast. Although they came from all over the world, some of these students had heard of us through my contacts in Germany. They included a Swiss medical student, Peter Czerny, who ended up marrying a local nurse who was an original "women's libber" and hippie "Creeker." She returned with him to Europe where they raised a family and she became thoroughly entrenched in Swiss culture. Unfortunately, our foreign student program eventually had to be discontinued when we were advised by our legal council that, since the students were not under the auspices of the University of British Columbia, if something went wrong, the hospital would be liable for any mistakes that were made. Even if the student did not perform the surgery, their presence in the operating room increased our liability. To this day, however, Sunshine Coast doctors continue to provide medical and surgical training opportunities for interns from medical schools across Canada.

Among the surgeries I performed in the early 1970s was an emergency operation on a teenage girl who had sustained a head injury. She had all of the signs and symptoms of a subdural hematoma, which is a collection of blood between the outer and middle layers of the brain. It was late at night, and time was of the essence if a death was to be prevented. I knew she would not survive a transfer to Vancouver, which even by helicopter would have taken two to three hours, so with a fair degree of trepidation I did the only thing possible to save her— I drilled a burr hole in her skull to drain the blood clot. This strategy worked and we were then able to transfer her to a Vancouver hospital where the family was told that I had saved her life. However, a house officer there also informed them that, because I had made the incision a bit too low, she would have a scar that would always be visible. As a result, some months later I received a notice that the family was suing me. Fortunately the action was dropped. It did, however, leave me with a bad taste in my mouth.

A somewhat lighter lawsuit was filed by a sixty-year-old whose cancer had necessitated the amputation of his left foot. We had been on friendly terms and he had phoned me to explain that, although I was not his main doctor, his lawyer had advised him to include everyone who had treated him in the lawsuit. While preparing me for the "discovery" hearing, my lawyer told me not to speculate and to make absolutely no jokes. The plaintiff's lawyer, a very prim and proper young woman entered the courtroom and was followed by the plaintiff. We greeted each other in a friendly manner and forgetting my lawyer's advice, I said, "Tom, you don't look any different, even though you're a foot shorter!" Even the man's lawyer managed a chuckle.

Early on the morning of New Year's Day 1972, I was called to the emergency room to attend a young teenager who had slashed her wrist at a ceremony she and her friends were having. She had done a good job, severing ten tendons, one nerve and an artery, and Denis Rogers and I spent over five hours in the operating room repairing the damage. We both felt the surgery ended surprisingly well and anticipated that the girl would regain full use of her hand. After six months of physical rehabilitation, she returned to my office for a follow-up examination, and I was pleased to see that the nerve was starting to function once more and she was demonstrating reasonable movement of her hand.

"How about moving your index finger," I suggested.

The girl flexed her thumb.

"Okay," I said, "now move your thumb."

When she flexed her index finger instead, I asked, "What do you think is going on?"

She looked at me then slowly grinned. "I think you hooked me up wrong, Doctor."

I then gave her the option of redoing the surgery and attaching the tendons correctly, or retraining her brain when she gave instructions to her thumb and index finger. She decided to retrain her brain.

Some time after this, the well-known local writer Hubert Evans, who wrote the classic novel *O Time in Your Flight*, came into my office. At age fifteen he had developed abdominal hernias, and doctors at that time—circa 1900—had told him that the operation was dangerous and he might die on the table. For the next sixty years he had worn trusses to retain the hernia within his abdominal cavity. On this visit to my office I said, "How about coming to the hospital so I can fix those hernias for you?" Hubert consented to have the surgery under spinal anaesthesia. The procedure was a success and the man was able to discard his trusses for good.

Before repairing an equally easy hernia presented by a lovely, elderly man named Alfred, I explained that there was a four percent chance of recurrence. When it did recur, he began describing himself a "four-percenter." I operated again, but the hernia recurred for a second time. Human nature would dictate that the man would now request another surgeon, and in anticipation of this, I made arrangements to send him to a colleague in Vancouver.

"Oh, no, Doctor!" Alfred said with a slow grin. "You're going to do this until you get it right." And I did.

Not every patient was as trusting as Alfred. One day in midsummer I was fishing when I received an urgent message from Dr. Roy Cline to get to the ER *stat!* "Don't change clothes—just get there!" he ordered.

The patient, a university professor, had sustained major injuries in a motor vehicle accident, and within minutes I could see that he needed urgent surgery or he would die. I explained this to his uninjured wife and she asked if we could get him to Vancouver.

"There's no time," I told her and gave the same response when she asked if a doctor could be sent here from Vancouver.

"Then," she asked, "could we get the best surgeon on the peninsula?"

Without meaning to be cruel and forgetting that in my fishing clothes I was really scruffy-looking, I said, "You're looking at him!"

When her jaw dropped, I felt bad for my remark. Fortunately, the surgery turned out well and we became great friends. They lived on the Sunshine Coast part-time and eventually switched their medical care to Dr. Gerring, who had given the anaesthetic. The patient's wife told me later that she knew the operation had turned out well when I came up to her casually in the waiting room with a cup of coffee in my hand.

There were times, however, when a surgery, though perfectly executed, came with consequences that were unacceptable to my patient. A quiet, elderly native gentleman had developed colon cancer, and as part of his treatment I performed a colostomy. I felt I had done an excellent job, and for three days following his surgery the man's recovery went well. On the third day, he had his first look at the stoma through which his feces would now be discharged and suddenly realized that he would have to deal with this for the rest of his life. Lying back against his pillow, he shook his head in resignation and said, "It's time for me to die, Doctor."

"You're doing fine," I consoled him. "You'll get used to this in no time."

The man didn't argue. Instead, he gently folded his hands across his chest and smiled. Within four days he was dead.

It was during that winter that I discovered an unexpected fringe benefit to being the only fully qualified surgeon on the Sunshine Coast. We had moved to our new house higher up the hill in Selma Park, and one night we had a huge snowstorm. The next morning I received an emergency call from the hospital, but because our road had not been ploughed, I was unable to get out with my car. Fortunately, I was able to walk to the hospital and arrived in time to deal with the emergency, but the incident caused such consternation at the hospital that the board of directors called the highways department and asked if they could keep my road open whenever there was a snow-storm. Thus, for many years, any time there was the slight-est snowfall, our road was cleaned first, a luxury that my six neighbours appreciated.

In 1966 my parents had moved to Richmond, BC, to be nearer to us, and since then we had spent a lot of time together. Dad and I enjoyed each other's company, and though he still never let me beat him at chess, we liked discussing each other's projects.

Although I had never qualified for any of Dad's choirs, clas-sical music has always been an important part of my home life as I find it very emotional and like to hear it played very loudly. One of my favourite old masters is Gustav Mahler, who was a very complex kind of composer, and I was listening to his music one afternoon while my father was visiting us.

"You like Mahler?" he asked, somewhat surprised.

"Oh, yeah," I responded. "I love Mahler!"

Dad wasn't impressed. "You're not musically sophisticated enough to appreciate him," he said with some amusement.

It was a shock for me when in June 1972, while Dad was loading his car for a trip, he suffered a massive heart attack and was rushed to the hospital. The next ten days were critical, but gradually he improved to the point where he was scheduled for discharge, and on my last visit to him we were talking about all the things he would do when he got home. That night Bonnie and I were roused from sleep by the phone ringing. It was the cardiologist calling to say that Dad had suffered a second heart attack and they hadn't been able to save him. While lying there digesting the news, Bonnie, who was four months pregnant, felt the baby move for the first time. "If it's a boy," she said softly, "we'll call him David after your dad."

With his passing, the Mennonite church community in Vancouver lost a valuable member for, as was his custom, he had become a choir conductor there and had been very involved in his community's musical life. His death also meant that I now had to look after my mother, whose grasp of English had not improved over the years. As well, my father had always taken care of the business side of their life. (He had never been able to understand why I knew nothing about my finances, and just shook his head when I said, "Well, Bonnie does all that.") Over the next few months we helped Mom sell their house and move into a Vancouver apartment block where a number of other Mennonite people lived. It was close to a Mennonite church where she soon made friends, and she lived there for many more years surrounded by companions with whom she shared the same language and customs.

Of course, in between dealing with my father's funeral and settling my mother's affairs, I still had to pay careful attention to my surgical practice, and one day, just a few weeks after Dad's funeral, I was called to the emergency ward to look after a patient who had been shot in the chest. Gerald and his family had been under my care since shortly after my arrival at Garden Bay. He was ten years older than his twenty-four-year-old wife, and the couple had six children, including two that I had delivered. Gerald was abusive in every sense of the word—physically assaulting his children, beating his wife, and running her down mentally and emotionally. Sometimes he would bring another woman into the house, lock himself in the bedroom with her and tell his wife—at the peril of another beating—not to bother them. She was a long-suffering, gentle kind of person who put up with the abuse because she had nowhere to turn. She had no money and was in such dire straits that she didn't even have a washing machine and had to rinse the baby's diapers in the bathtub and hang them up to dry in the house.

In an odd twist of fate, Gerald's widowed mother married

his wife's widowed father, Rayner. He was disabled and often bedridden and she suffered from her own health problems, so the two lived on a disability pension and were virtually house-bound. Whenever their pension cheques arrived, Gerald would show up at the house and force his mother to sign hers over to him. He would then cash the cheque, keeping most of the money for himself and giving the old people barely enough to live on. Then one day Gerald's mother refused to sign the cheque, and he began to beat her. When Rayner yelled at him from the bedroom, he charged in there ready to pummel his stepdad as well. Only this time Rayner was waiting for him with a rifle.

Jim Hobson was the first to arrive on the scene and was kneeling over Gerald, who was still alive, when he heard a click behind his ear and a cold voice said, "Don't move!" Jim looked slowly around and discovered a very nervous-looking young police officer holding a revolver on him. He had thought Jim was the perpetrator of the deed and felt pretty bad when he recognized the doctor.

Gerald was transported to the hospital, and although we did our best, we were unable to save him. Consequently, his stepfather was charged with non-capital murder, and the case eventually went to the BC Supreme Court. In his testimony, backed by that of his wife, Rayner claimed that on hearing a commotion in the kitchen he had grabbed his rifle and swung off his bed, coming down on his bad leg. As he stumbled to-wards the other room, he saw Gerald standing over his mother with his fist clenched. In that moment, Rayner fell and his trig-ger hand struck the door jam, causing the rifle to fire.

"I was as much surprised as anyone when that happened," Rayner declared.[28]

The defence lawyer brought in a great number of charac-ter witnesses from Roberts Creek, all of whom spoke in glow-ing terms of Rayner. No one, not even his widow or children, would give a character reference for the deceased.

This story had a happy ending, for the Supreme Court found Rayner not guilty, and a short while later a very kind retired logger fell in love with Gerald's widow. After they were married, they moved to the interior of BC where he helped raise her children.

Dealing with death, even the death of someone as abusive as Gerald, is a stressful business for medical professionals, and while some, like myself, are able to separate our private lives from most of what happens at the hospital, there are certain tragedies that stay with us for a long time. One of our coping strategies is to have occasional parties and get-togethers, which balance the tragic side of our work with some good, uninhibited fun. Among my favourite traditions of the past was our annual operating room Christmas party, which was characterized by a mix of home-made skits, poems, songs and laughter. One year the party was held at ten a.m. in the recovery suite, and Walter Burtnick and I were competing to be the best decorated Christmas tree. We each had a team to apply our decorations, and my group was comprised of three lady doctors who lavish-

Unflappable and always cheerful, our next supervisor, Marge Mackenzie (Auntie Marge) ran a smooth operation.

ly adorned me with flashing lights, lipstick and tinsel. They had just finished decking me out in royal splendour when our festivities were interrupted by an order over the intercom.

"Dr. Paetkau, to the ER. Stat!"

Figuring this page was all part of the fun, I marched proudly down the hall to the emergency room and was immediately ushered to a bedside where I stared down at the terrified face of my patient, Jim, who was clutching

One of our favourite traditions at St. Mary's Hospital was the operating room Christmas party. The nurses improvised, and there was a mix of home-made skits, poems, songs and laughter.

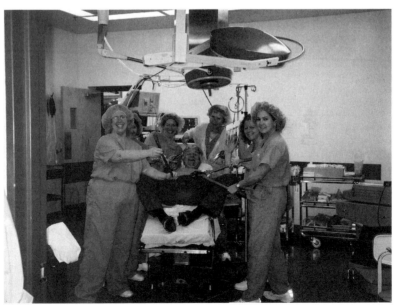

Some of the angels of St. Mary's Hospital pose with the author. Our occasional get-togethers helped balance the sometimes tragic side of our work with good, uninhibited fun.

a sheet of skin that was preventing his guts from falling out. He had been working at one of the local sawmills when his saw had malfunctioned and the blade had flown off, literally slicing off his abdominal wall so it was hanging on by only a small bridge of skin. Somehow he had managed to put the wall back into place and hold it there as he was transported to the hospital. He and his wife were both distraught and I can only imagine what they thought when they saw their surgeon decked out like a Christmas tree! Obviously they weren't reassured.

I took one look at him and said, "Get him to the O.R. Stat!" Then I ran out.

Although there were unavoidable complications, Jim survived his surgery and recovered. The following Christmas he and his wife were invited as special guests to our party, and they had a great time recounting the story of how a decorated surgeon came to his bedside.

Another skit was the result of a question by one of our nurses, "Auntie" Marge Mackenzie. I had been repairing a hernia on a teenaged boy when she asked how the young man had

Thorne Duncan (left) was a master of many occupations including hand-logging on Texada Island. His wife Lewella was Garden Bay Hospital's true blue receptionist.

discovered his hernia. When I told her that his girlfriend had found it, Marge shushed and admonished me to get serious for a change. At that year's Christmas party I got Marge's teenaged son Keith to lie on a stretcher completely covered up, while one of the nurses, pretending to be his mother, came up and said sternly, "Get out of bed, you lazy kid! It's time to go to school."

As he had been instructed, Keith sat up and said, "Mom, what's a hernia?"

I thought Marge was going to pass out laughing and blushing.

But Marge got her own back. Many years later as I was watching our new OB/GYN doctor, Russ Kellett, performing an operation I used to do, she noticed my pensive expression and said, "You don't like someone else fishing in your stream, do you, E.P.?"

For me hunting trips were another way to deal with stress levels, and they began when Bonnie and I were still living at Garden Bay. Thorne and Lewella Duncan had invited us to dinner one night and served a feast of wild game, shrimp and fish. Thorne was a master of many occupations including hand-logging on Texada Island, fishing up the central coast and trapping on Nelson Island. Every fall he also went on a hunting trip, and when I showed an interest, he invited me along on a fall trip. We drove with two other men to a ranch at Punchesakut, which is about five hours west of Quesnel. The owner of the ranch was an outfitter, guide and accomplished outdoorsman, well-educated and well-read, and he loved classical music. We got a couple of moose on that trip and I proudly brought my allotted quarter home to Bonnie. She was not impressed.

"What are you going to do with it?" she asked. "I won't eat it and neither will the kids."

Fortunately, the local Rod and Gun Club were having their annual game banquet that weekend and were delighted to take it off my hands.

Sadly, while I was in Germany, Thorne was hit by a tree he was falling with his partner, Bert Gooldrup, on Texada Island. Noting that the tree was coming down the wrong way, he had crouched behind a big boulder, but the tree was rotten and when it hit the rock a section broke off and hit him in the neck. Although he knew he was in trouble, he was still able to walk, so with Bert's help he made it down to the boat and they headed for Garden Bay. After they docked, Bert ran up to get Al

Swan, but by the time they got back to the boat, Thorne was dead. The autopsy showed that he had fractured his neck, and while he was waiting in the boat for the doctor, he must have turned his head and severed the cord.

After that I hunted with Red Nicholson, and on one trip we stayed with a friend who owned a ranch in the Chilcotin. In the midst of our stay the rancher's bull was brought off the range with advanced "pink eye." This was a $5,000 animal and the rancher was distraught because he was going to have to put him down.

"Why don't I take the eye out?" I suggested.

With nothing to lose, the rancher agreed. The next day he put the bull in a restrictive chute and I began the surgery. By this time word had spread about what I was going to do, and all of the local ranchers were there, leaning on the rails, to observe as I injected a local anaesthetic and then proceeded to carve the eye out with a hunting knife. Watching the procedure, one young lady asked breathlessly, "Is he really a doctor?"

"He sure is!" said Red proudly.

The lady responded, "Boy, I'd never go to him!"

There was always great camaraderie among the men who shared these trips, and I enjoyed it so much that I continued to go along even when I stopped shooting game. Now I spend my time looking at animals through binoculars and let the others do the hunting. Walter Burtnick used to say that if we spent an equal amount of money on gas, booze and food on one of these trips, it was a success.

Since my early days at Hay River, fishing had been a stress reliever for me and shortly after we moved to Garden Bay, Red Nicholson took me under his wing and showed me how to fish in the salt chuck. At that time fishing here was still great, and during the summer the waters of Lees Bay, Pender Harbour and across to Nelson Island would be filled with hundreds of boats. Margaret Bolderson, who worked at our clinic, and her husband, Roy, lived in a house with a verandah that extended out over the water and was supported by stilts. From here they would jig for herring, then cast the line out with herring for bait and get a bigger fish. Although Walter Burtnick and Red did try to introduce me to freshwater fishing and fly casting, I never got the same thrill out of that as I do when I'm out on the salt chuck and hear that line go *zing!* without knowing what's on the end of it until the fish is actually landed.

For the past fifteen years my fishing has been limited to an annual trip that my daughter Carla's father-in-law, Mack Bryson, and I take to the Black Gold Lodge at the mouth of Rivers Inlet. This tradition began while Mack and I were visiting with my friend and patient Howard Jones who was the superintendent of a logging camp in that area. After inviting Mack and me to accompany him to the lodge where he had to attend a meeting, Howard persuaded the lodge owner, Jim Rough, to take us out fishing. Jim was a little hostile over the imposition, but he took us to a fishing hole and started handing out gear. When I went to bait my hook, however, he said

Since my early days working with the Fisheries Research Board in the Northwest Territories, fishing had been a stress reliever for me, and after our arrival in Garden Bay, Red Nicholson took me under his wing.

sharply, "No! Don't touch anything. I'll do it all." He then put the bait on my hook, flipped the line into the water, reeled off several feet, and handed the rod to me. As soon as I took it, the line just screamed out—a huge salmon had taken the bait. We caught that one and several others, and while we were fishing we got to talking about hunting. It turned out that Jim was a trophy hunter and had gone all over the world in search of game. When Mack told him that he had once owned the Empire Valley Ranch and still had connections with it, Jim was impressed and readily agreed when Mack invited him to go on our next hunting trip.

That November Mack phoned Jim.

"Jim? This is Mack Bryson. I wanted to invite you . . . ."

"Who?"

"Mack Bryson."

"Who?"

"Listen," Mack said, "do you want to go hunting on the Empire Valley Ranch?"

"Jesus Christ!" Jim exploded. "I never thought you'd call!"

Jim and I really bonded on that hunting trip, and since then Mack and I have been going to his lodge at Rivers Inlet every summer. One year just after our plane docked, Jim's wife, Brenda, came running out.

"Jim's in trouble!" she cried.

We hurried into the lodge where Jim was suffering a vasovagal attack, a situation that occurs when the heart slows down so much that the victim faints. I'm sure Jim would have come around on his own, but because I was there to help, he believes I saved his life. I didn't try too hard to dissuade him. At any rate, our plane was still at the dock so I took him to the hospital at Port Hardy, and after some testing it was decided to send him to New Westminster where they found he needed a pacemaker. After that day, Jim has insisted that we come as his guests every year.

CHAPTER 7

Vote Early, Vote Often

The quality of care provided by Canadian hospitals is determined by the Canadian Council on Hospital Accreditation (CCHA) through a voluntary accreditation process that is free from government intervention and conducted every three years. Using specially designed questionnaires, the hospital's entire staff collects information on buildings and equipment, on the functioning of the hospital overall, and on the quality of care given to patients. After the staff assesses this data, the CCHA appoints an independent surveyor, usually a physician and/or a nurse from another hospital, to complete a survey, analyze the data and make a report that includes recommendations for improvements.[29]

Our hospital administrator, Ellen Bragg, believed that accreditation was necessary not only to attract top-quality staff to our hospital but also to obtain the financing we needed to operate efficiently. Under her direction, the staff had completed the application process in both 1972 and 1973 but only achieved provisional accreditation. In 1974 we tried again, this time diligently making the improvements the previous surveyors had suggested, and, as before, gathering the required information, completing the questionnaires and evaluating our overall hospital procedures and nursing practices. With seventy-one beds, one hundred and twenty staff and ten full-time physicians, this involved a lot of extra work, but everyone pulled together. Consultants were invited into each department to provide input on improving practices both for cost and efficiency. Some of these experts came from UBC, the BC Department of Health, the BC Medical Association, and the Registered Nurses Association of BC, as well as from other hospitals such as St. Paul's, Vancouver General and Lions Gate. Finally, after a thorough inspection on August 16, 1974, by a CCHA physician surveyor and a CCHA nurse surveyor, we became the sixty-sixth hospital in BC (out of one hundred and twenty) to become fully accredited.[30]

Unfortunately, our glow of accomplishment was soon overshadowed by discontent within the community for circumstances that were beyond our control. Although we had gained fifteen additional acute care beds and twenty beds for extended care just three years earlier, there had been no simultaneous expansion of the x-ray, laboratory, engineering or administration areas, and by 1975 workloads had doubled in these departments. Overcrowding caused by the addition of new equipment as well as awkward working spaces was slowing down service. Patient privacy was compromised as surgical daycare patients were placed on stretchers in a curtained-off part of emergency, and there were no suitable waiting areas for relatives and friends of patients.[31]

At the same time, however, Ellen Bragg was bringing together various organizations within the community, such as public health workers, seniors groups, probation officers, social workers and mental health workers, to co-ordinate their efforts with each other and the hospital. By 1974 this group, registered as the Sunshine Coast Community Resource Society, was providing daycare, homemaker assistance, a telephone tree and information services, as well as a mini-bus to transport passengers to hospitals, medical clinics, daycare and recreation facilities for patients in the hospital's extended care ward. They were also involved in planning for intermediate care facilities within the community.[32] At the same time, to improve our service at the medical clinics, we had begun stationing a doctor at the hospital from six o'clock every evening until eight o'clock the next morning. This system was also good for us doctors for it meant that our emergency duty hours were reduced from once every fourth night (generally preceded and followed by normal shifts at the clinic) to once every eighth night.[33]

Meanwhile, as both chief of staff at the hospital and manager of our Sechelt clinic, I had been no stranger to government bureaucracy. Frustrated by the money that was being wasted in the medical field, I had shared my ideas for cutting costs with officials from the Ministry of Health. Their response was that we didn't have to worry about saving money because "in BC we have an embarrassment of riches."

This was not my first political experience. I had been involved in regional district politics through the Sunshine Coast Recreation Committee, which had been campaigning since 1967 for a centralized community centre on Lot 1506 in Roberts Creek. Eric Hensch and I had been chosen by the Sechelt Lions Club to get the project going. A road was built into the site free of charge by Pete Jackson, Rudy Crucil, the Fieldling brothers and other volunteers, and we prepared for a public referendum. Since a 60 percent "yes" vote was required to win, Eric and I campaigned hard, giving speeches in eighteen community centres on the coast, but we received only 58 percent of the votes. We learned later that summer cottagers, who did not want to see their taxes increased, had actually rented a bus to come up and vote "no." So we tried again and this time I asked the McNevins, who were movers and shakers in the union movement, to arrange for a wildcat ferry strike on the day of the referendum. Of course, this didn't happen and we were defeated once more. Then in 1972 the new NDP government reduced the passing requirement to a 50 percent "yes" vote. Certain that we would now be successful, we applied for a third referendum but this time failed to obtain Sechelt's support; having accepted a proposal from Henry Hall, a private contractor, to build an arena in the West Porpoise Bay area without any increase in taxation, the people of Sechelt were no longer interested in a centralized community facility. The only good outcome from this exercise was that, through an exchange with MacMillan Bloedel, we stopped the Sunshine Coast Golf and Country Club from gobbling up this 115-acre property, and it is now the wonderland of wooded trails, picnic areas and playing fields known as Cliff Gilker Park.

My involvement in politics, however, had not been limited to medical costs and recreation centres. While the NDP, led by Dave Barrett, were in power, there were a number of issues that concerned me about the way they were managing the affairs of British Columbia.[34] When it was suggested to me that I could do something about these issues, I remembered my father al-

ways telling me to stand up for what I believed. I was already accustomed to making decisions and taking responsibility on a one-to-one basis for a lot of critical things in medicine. *Maybe*, I thought, *I can help a lot of people by becoming involved in politics and putting forward my ideas about responsibility and restraint.* I had witnessed the shouting and disorderly conduct of the legislature in Victoria, and I was sure I could do better than that.[35] So in mid-September 1975 I announced that I would seek the Social Credit nomination for the Mackenzie Riding, which in those days

Those five weeks as a would-be politician were heady times, but I soon found that the people I encountered were entrenched in their own ideas—very few changed their minds during the course of the campaign.

extended from the end of Dean Channel, northwest of Bella Coola, almost to the edge of Tweedsmuir Park, and south to Howe Sound and the Sunshine Coast and included Ocean Falls as well as Smith, Rivers and Seymour inlets and the islands of the Broughton Archipelago. My opponents for the nomination were Peter Prescesky of Madeira Park and Ted Cooper of Powell River. By November 3, when Barrett called a provincial election for December 11, I was already caught up in a whirlwind of speaking engagements and campaigning. However, when I won the nomination, I was pretty certain that it wasn't necessarily party support that elected me, but rather the number of friends and acquaintances I had made through my medical practice and my involvement in the community. Still, I was charged with enthusiasm as I headed into the provincial campaign, armed with fresh ideas and a determination to keep my expenses under the $12,000 budget we had allotted for our riding. (Consistent with my platform of fiscal responsibility, this was $2,000 less than the budget in the previous election.) Running against me in the provincial campaign was the NDP incumbent, Don Lockstead, and the Conservative candidate, Guy Harrington.[36] Lil Fraser, my campaign manager, was a real ball of fire, and although I don't think she'd ever done anything of this magnitude, she was a great organizer and helped me to plan my strategies. She understood that my goal of becoming an MLA was not to obtain a cabinet post, but to contribute as a back bencher, getting involved in all kinds of committee work. As a Type A personality, I work well under pressure, and I was sure that I could do whatever job was given to me.[37]

With the idealism of the untried, I went into the campaign promising a common sense approach that promoted restraint, responsibility and individual liberty. In the medical field, I hoped to institute the use of paramedical people who would cut a doctor's workload. Both government and doctors favoured this idea, but no one wanted to be responsible for establishing such a program because they might be sued. I also proposed an alternative to our ambulance service for patients who did not need to lie down and thus eliminate the costly requirement for two attendants. I outlined strategies for patients who were mobile and in no danger of transmitting or contracting an infectious condition to stay in self-care units where they could do their own housekeeping, go to the nurses' station for their medications and to the cafeteria for their meals.[38] Building extended care homes was another one of my proposals, but in that I was definitely ahead of my time.

Many of my ideas came from my personal experience with the Kaiser health care system in California. Under this private health plan, care was broken down into tiers. When a patient phoned the health care unit, a triage nurse would determine whether to send a nurse, which would cost the least, or a doctor, which would cost more, or if an ambulance should be sent. In this way, while cost was certainly a factor, an appropriate service was still provided.

As an avid sports fisherman, I was interested, too, in safeguarding our wild fishery. Over the summer, through an Opportunity for Youth project, several creeks on the Sunshine Coast had been cleared of log jams and other debris, and cement baffles had been installed on a creek at Williamson's Landing. In November the Gibsons' Wildlife Club had announced that they would be investigating the possibility of establishing a salmon enhancement program on the coast. If I was elected, it was programs like this that I wanted to support.[39]

My idealism, however, was met with tolerant smiles from more experienced politicians, and I remember Dan Campbell, who had been the Minister of Municipal Affairs in W.A.C. Bennett's cabinet, saying, "Eric, if you get in, be prepared not to accomplish very much. Nothing happens overnight. The wheels turn slowly and the idealists don't get anywhere."

One of the greatest surprises I encountered in my campaign was discovering how entrenched people are in their ideas. To me it seemed that a perfect way around the impasses occurring between labour and management in those days was to give the employees a piece of the action. Then if a business profited, everyone would share in the profits. I had seen how well this policy had worked with my friends, the Matsons, who ran Bear Bay Logging on Jervis Inlet. The men from their camp had refused to sign up with any union, and when I had asked them about this, they all said there was no need for a union. "We get union wages," one man told me, "and at the end of the year, we get a Christmas bonus. The food in our camp is the best in the world. There is no cutting costs by using powdered milk— fresh milk, fruit and vegetables are flown in twice a week. If we joined the union, all that would change."

With this in mind, I went to the union leaders both at Port Mellon and in Powell River, and asked, "Why don't you guys ask for a profit-sharing arrangement?" The men said they weren't interested. They just wanted wages and benefits, not part of the company. Here, too, I discovered that taking a political stand created instant antagonism, and when I went among the union members, many of whom had been my patients at one time or another, there was suddenly no friendly, "Hey, Eric!" Instead there was tangible hostility, and I eventually realized there was not much I could do about that.

People didn't seem to understand the issues that were being debated, and they weren't interested in listening to the candidates' views. I believe most of them had already decided how they were going to vote, and very few changed their minds during the course of the campaign. Even some of my friends were caught up in partisan politics, and I remember asking one who had been an NDP supporter all of his life, "How about voting for me this time?"

"Eric," he said, "if Donald Duck were running for the NDP, I'd still vote for him. It's in the blood."

For many of my patients, however, the concern was not whether I agreed with their political views or could make a difference in government. They were worried that they would lose me as a doctor and for that reason some even wrote letters to the editor of the local paper urging people not to vote for me.[40] Still, those five weeks were heady times, and I found myself being caught up in the atmosphere of power, going to meetings with Bill Bennett and other high-ranking politicians and visiting communities that I'd never even heard of before. On one of my trips to some of the more remote settlements, Al Campbell donated a plane and the pilot, Don Sutherland, donated his time. Near Bella Bella we passed over a small bay where a gyppo logger was working, and although my time was limited, we decided to touch down there just to say hello to the man and his family. They were a really nice Scandinavian couple with two teenaged children, and being isolated, they welcomed our visit. Unfortunately, while we conversed over coffee, a storm came in that made leaving impossible, so instead of flying in and out for a two-hour stopover, we spent two nights with the family. Although they were NDP supporters, I believe they both voted for me, but it was a very time-consuming way to get a couple of votes.

Shortly after that I visited Ocean Falls, a town created in 1906 to provide homes for the employees of a pulp and paper mill, which was for a long time the largest in BC. In the early 1970s, a plan by owners Crown Zellerbach to phase out the mill due to its old facilities and high operating costs was averted when the NDP government bought the entire town and established the Ocean Falls Corporation to run the mill. The morning I arrived, Don Lockstead's campaign manager, Joanne McNevin, was already there. We were both on the board of directors for St. Mary's Hospital, and although we kidded each other, our political differences had never got in the way of our friendship. I joined her for breakfast at the local hotel, and after sharing a laugh at the coincidence of our arriving at the same time, she said, "Well, Eric, you're wasting your time. All of the votes in this town are going to go to Don Lockstead."

I said, "Well, whatever."

"You know," she said, "you're running for the wrong party." Of course, I didn't agree, but I was to discover later that as far as Ocean Falls was concerned, she was right.

For me the climax of the campaign was a debate sponsored by the Christian Action Committee of Vancouver that was held on December 2 at the PNE Agrodome, when the four provincial party leaders shared the platform. There were fifty-two candidates in attendance along with six thousand partisan supporters, including a lot of people from the Sunshine Coast, and many were carrying placards. The place was alive with music and speeches and cheering, and I was right in the middle of it.[41]

In my own race in the riding of Mackenzie, the Progressive Conservative candidate, Guy Harrington, withdrew in late November, and soon after that Liberal candidate Marion McRae entered the fray. One night the two of us matched wits in front of a crowd at the Assumption Catholic School in Powell River, and among the questions put to us was one asking for our views on abortion. McRae's challenge to me on this issue and my response were reported in *The Peninsula Times*:

> Standing up, McRae said, "As I am the only candidate who could have an abortion, I will ask Dr. Paetkau how he would control my life."
>
> Paetkau, a surgeon, replied, "I personally don't do abortions. I have five children and believe that life is a straight line from conception to death. There is nothing that can be done on a provincial level as it is up to the federal government. It is a matter between doctor and patient. It is hard to legislate life and death or religion. So, my fellow candidate, I wouldn't do anything to you."[42]

On election night a party for Social Credit supporters was held at the Parthenon Restaurant in Sechelt. It was supposed to be a victory party, and when Bonnie and I arrived just before the election results began to come in, the atmosphere was optimistic. We stayed for an hour and then went to the Social Credit headquarters in Sechelt to watch the returns on television. Don Lockstead, who was in the lead from the beginning, gained steadily and by 8:45 it was clear that he was going to be returned as the MLA for this riding. I received the news with mixed emotions. I had been so sure of winning that I felt as if I'd received a sock in the eye, and yet a part of me was relieved.

"How can I be dismayed?" I asked the *Peninsula Times* reporter covering the Social Credit headquarters. "That's a tough job, going to Victoria. It would have been a great disruption to my life; I wasn't looking forward to it. I've got a great job and I don't mind staying in Sechelt. I'm satisfied. It looks like the best man won. My family will be pleased they'll be keeping me home."[43]

After admitting defeat, I telephoned Don Lockstead, who was celebrating in Powell River, to congratulate him. His response was to thank me for running a clean campaign and to promise me that he would quit smoking. He also quipped that the Sunshine Coast had gained a fine surgeon.[44]

Looking back, I realize there were many reasons why I didn't win the election, aside from the fact that I was running against a well-entrenched incumbent. For one thing, I was a newcomer to politics and I don't believe people saw me as a legislator. Of course, winning is in my blood, and I didn't like the fact that I lost the election, but I realized I might have been taking on more responsibility than I was prepared for. As an MLA I would have had to travel from community to community within this vast area, as well as spending time in the legislature and in dealing with the problems of local constituents, drastically cutting the time I could spend with my family and my medical practice.

So, when it was all over and ballot boxes were stowed away, I went back to being a surgeon, feeling the whole thing had turned out well: the Socreds got in and I didn't.

CHAPTER 8

Definitely Older, Maybe Wiser

In the 1960s, it had still been customary for doctors to make a long-term commitment to their community by investing in their own homes and office buildings. It was for this reason that our partnership, which by 1964 included Al Swan, Walter Burtnick, Jim Hobson and myself, had purchased property at the corner of Wharf and Cowrie on which to build our own clinic. However, before construction started, we rented a new building owned by Werner and Annaleis Richter at the corner of Inlet Avenue and Mermaid Street. Eventually the Richters were persuaded to sell us the building. As well, in 1968 we had purchased property on Highway 101 in Gibsons and constructed a new clinic there. Within a few years after this new Gibsons clinic opened, our medical staff there included Dr. R.A. Cline and Dr. Mark Mountain. And when a Dr. Granger Avery was looking for a job, I wanted to hire him sight unseen. I emvisioned the receptionist answering the phone, "Drs. Cline, Avery, Mountain . . ."

By the mid-1970s there were eleven doctors working out of these two clinics, so that we now needed management teams, one for each location, but our income and expenses continued to be divided equally among all the doctors and spread out over five years so that we could each take a paid sabbatical every fifth year. Now, however, some of the new partners were expressing concerns that the system was not fair to everyone. As the only surgeon, I was bringing in more money than anyone else and worked harder because I was on call all the time, and although I had made no complaints about this, it was becoming clear that each doctor worked at his own pace. Some would spend an hour with each patient, bringing in very little income, yet they received the same share as doctors who were contributing much more than that. Consequently, a meeting was called, and after some discussion it was decided that instead of being partners, each doctor would become an associate, and the distribution of income was changed to a more equitable arrangement while still maintaining our sabbatical system.

Around this same time one of my best friends from my residency years in San Francisco phoned to say that he had a terminal illness. We had often skied together and our families had visited back and forth, and when he asked if I could come and visit with him before he died, I wanted to drop everything and fly down there. Unfortunately, it was impossible for either myself or Bonnie to get away, but we did a lot of phoning back and forth. One day he said, "I wish we'd had more time together, Eric. People should make more time for each other, so when they're going to die, they don't have any regrets about that."

I decided that I never wanted to find myself in the position, when it was too late to do anything about it, of wishing I had visited more often with my friends. Al Swan, Walter Burtnick and I had already addressed this issue in a small way. Although we had been good friends right from the beginning, our practice was always so busy that we had never been able to spend a lot of time together, partly because we felt that one of us always had to be available at the clinic. In the late 1960s, however, we started treating ourselves to a trip every fall, and our friendship deepened even more, and after my San Francisco friend died, I began arranging a weekly lunch date with Al,

From left to right: Marsh Rae, Harold Clay, Red Nicholson, Walter Burtnick, and Alan Swan. We would meet every Friday for lunch at the Wakefield Inn, where we solved all the world's problems, and it gradually became a long-running tradition.

Walter, Denis Rogers and five other close friends. We would meet at the Wakefield Inn every Friday for lunch and it gradually became such a tradition that the Radimskys, who owned the inn, would automatically reserve the same table for us. Of course, by this time Al, Walter and I were the old-timers, and while the younger doctors liked to come and listen to our stories around the table, we were no longer the movers and shakers, as it were.

Al Swan was a frugal man with a deeply religious upbringing, and it had always been his intention to do missionary work when his children were grown. Thus, in May 1976 when his daughter Eleanor graduated from UBC and his two sons were eighteen and nineteen, he decided the time had come to make a life change. A month later, after serving the Sunshine Coast for twenty-two years, he retired from our medical practice.

Africa had been Al's first choice for his mission work, but because of the turmoil plaguing that continent, he turned his attention to areas closer to home. When a contact at the BC

College of Physicians and Surgeons told him that the Native people in northern BC were not being adequately looked after, he accepted a posting to Dease Lake.[45] From that base, every six weeks he and Rosa travelled from Telegraph Creek to Kincolith, Nishga, Kitkatla, Hartley Bay and Iskut. At each settlement, he worked with either the community doctor or the nurse practitioner, checking the practitioner's diagnoses, helping out with difficult cases or sending patients out to hospital.[46]

A month after Al's departure I went on my third and final sabbatical. Wanting to learn more about pathology, I had contacted the Kaiser Foundation Hospital in San Francisco and asked if I could do a year's work in pathology there, and because of my previous experience with them, they actually created a job for me in that department, providing that I would be available to do some surgery if required. With our children getting older, however, uprooting them from their lives here on the Sunshine Coast was not so easy, and at first the girls, who were now teenagers with summer jobs, rebelled then reluctantly agreed to join us in September. As usual, Bonnie organized the move, turned the house we rented in San Francisco into a home and arranged school admissions for the children.

Al Swan and Walter Burtnick—no longer the movers and shakers, now the storytellers.

In some ways, this was the best of my three sabbaticals, for while I was scheduled to work from nine to five, I was generally able to quit at four, and I was only on call every sixth weekend for emergency autopsies. These were limited to deaths involving a certain

Jewish sect, which believed that burial had to take place within forty-eight hours of death, and to deaths resulting from fulminating infections. Since neither situation occurred during my watch, I never once got called in. Consequently, Bonnie and I had a really great social life that year and we did many things together and as a family.

There were other ways, however, in which this was not such a good year, and one of these was due to the nature of my work. Part of the job was occasionally going to the city morgue with the pathologists from our hospital and doing autopsies on persons who had died the previous day—usually including about six violent deaths—and there were times when it was difficult for me to deal with these cases. This happened one day after I had just completed an autopsy on a very pretty twenty-year-old girl who had committed suicide by jumping off the Golden Gate Bridge. My next case was a six-year-old boy whose mother and her boyfriend had chained him to the toilet seat so he could drink but couldn't get away. They had fed him so little food that he developed *kwashiorkor*, an African word used to describe the enlarged liver and huge belly of a child suffering from starvation, and he finally died. I remember looking down at this little boy and making some very emotional comments about these two cases, when the deaner, who was a big black guy, said to me, "Doctah, they're just meat. You can't take all this to your heart." It was harsh, but it smartened me up and gave me the perspective I needed to continue with the autopsy.

During that sabbatical, Carla also had difficulties, which I didn't even know about at the time. Blonde and pretty, she was a real athlete and played many different sports, often against boys. One day after leaving a high school where she'd gone to play pick-up basketball with some other teenagers, she walked to a transit stop, and as she waited for a bus to take her home some of the guys she had just played basketball with came out onto the street. Seeing her standing by herself, they immediately went over and asked if she knew how dangerous it was for her to be there.

"You won't last on this corner!" they said and insisted on staying with her until she was safely on the bus.

Not too long after this she was walking down the hallway at George Washington High School when she saw a couple of big, tough-looking youths prying a door off with a crowbar. Being Carla, she was about to say something then remembered stories she'd heard of things that had happened in the corridors and under the stairwells of that school. Instead of protesting, she ignored what was happening and walked on by.

It was a tough school, but both she and Karin adapted.

Despite the drawbacks, we all liked living in San Francisco and when, at the end of my residency, I was offered a really good job at the hospital, we suddenly had to make up our minds whether we wanted to return to Sechelt or stay in San Francisco. To help us decide, we sat down as a family and each made a list of all the important things in our lives, rating them on a scale of one to ten. Sechelt won for everybody except Karin who wanted to go to university in California. For me, the lure of the wilderness that we have here and my garden were enough to make me say no to a great city and a new job.

We returned to Sechelt at the end of June 1977, and our lives picked up more or less where they had been before we left. Bonnie was kept busy looking after our five active children, and although she wasn't as involved with the Hospital Auxiliary as she had been in our early years on the coast, she continued to visit patients, distributing books and magazines, or just stopped to chat. She was much amused one day when an elderly gentleman whom she was visiting peered at her name tag and asked if she was the doctor's daughter.

With so much of my attention focussed on medical matters, I took her management of household and financial matters for granted and seldom carried any cash with me. In those long-ago days before debit and credit cards, this might have been a problem had we not been living in a town where everyone knew the local doctors. More than once I popped into George Flay's barber shop for a cut and realized after the job was complete that I couldn't pay the bill. A few days later Bonnie would be walking by on the street and George would call her over and say, "You owe me for Eric's haircut!" I found it most apt that, when they were once asked who was the boss in our family, one of our girls said, "Mom's the boss, but what Dad says goes."

Family time was important to both Bonnie and me, and because David and Mark were both really keen on hockey and were good at it, I got involved in the Minor Hockey League, first as team manager and then as a coach. Whenever I was able to be home, I'd shoot baskets with the kids or play hockey in the carport or catch out in the yard. To escape the interruptions that came with being on call all the time, we would often go off the coast for skiing and boating, to attend concerts or to go on extended vacations.

At dinner in order to find out what the kids did when we weren't around, we would give each one a turn to tell about his or her day. To encourage them to become independent, we gave them guidelines but allowed them the freedom to make their own decisions. So when Karin obtained her driver's licence, I said, "This is the only time I'm going to talk to you about this, but if you ever get caught drinking and driving or speeding, you won't get the car again. Don't even ask."

Some time later a Mountie, who was also a friend, said, "Eric, I want to tell you a story about your daughter. We were monitoring a party at Elphinstone and we saw Karin and five of her girlfriends get into your car. Your daughter was driving and we followed and pulled them over. The car reeked of beer, so I asked Karin to get out and walk the white line. When she completed the task successfully, I asked, 'Well, how much have you had to drink?' Karin said, 'Nothing. I've got my dad's car.' I still didn't trust the situation, so I said,

'Oh?' She looked at me and said, 'Listen, I'm more afraid of my dad than you!'"

Of course, our kids liked their modern music, and when they were teenagers, that's what they wanted to listen to. Sometimes, as I was parking the car on my return home, I would see one of the kids running over to the stereo and hear one of them shout, "Dad's home! Stop the music!"

For a while we joined with friends to raise pigs, using our acreage but sharing the expenses. The animals were named after the wives. Using a felt pen, I wrote our phone number on the sides of the wee piglets so that when they escaped, the neighbours would know who to phone. At butchering time George Sim, a retired butcher and haggis-maker, came over to help. We owned a backhoe at the time and used it to do the lifting and dunking. Daughter Carla proved so adept at handling the backhoe that George commented, "She could play the piano with it!"

The lure of the wilderness was enough to make me say no to a new job in San Francisco. We returned to Sechelt at the end of June 1977, and our family picked up more or less where we had left off.

Raising birds was another of my off-duty activities, a pursuit that started out innocently enough and then just seemed to keep expanding. It began when we went to an acreage in Gibsons to look at a horse for Guy. Although we didn't buy the horse, we did admire the owner's peacocks. "They're lovely birds," she said, "but they're destroying my flowers and making too much noise. Would you like to buy them?"

Remembering my days as a boy raising owls and collecting eggs, I thought this was a pretty good idea, so I constructed a large pen that opened into our barn and then collected the birds. Over the years I have built up an aviary of peacocks, pheasants, grouse, two kinds of doves, canaries and chickens, sharing the eggs with friends and family. They're beautiful birds and so tame that I can walk among them, yet if they hear a strange noise, they go crazy. I love to watch them interact and to see what transpires in the bird world, especially how they all get along, although it does get a bit noisy when the peacocks start honking. Of course, as always, Bonnie provides backup and takes on the job of looking after our "farm" when I'm away or on call.

In the late summer of 1974, our medical practice once again faced criticism from people in Pender Harbour who felt we were not providing them with adequate medical coverage. I had stopped going to our clinic in Madeira Park in 1969, and although Walter Burtnick had continued to man it one day a week, attendance was so low that eventually we closed it down. As soon as we did this, Pender Harbour residents began agitating for both a clinic and a full-time doctor. When a government official asked for our opinion on the subject, we recommended the construction of a subsidized doctor's office plus a twenty-four-hour-a-day telephone answering service and an ambulance, but repeated requests to the government for this were turned down. Finally, with the same independent community spirit and determination that had resulted in the establishment of the first hospital on the Sunshine Coast, the local residents got together to fundraise and build the Pender Harbour Health Centre, which was opened on December 8, 1976.

Eventually the government agreed to fund a doctor for the centre, paying $40,000 a year for a forty-hour week, plus benefits. However, since this doctor had to do rounds each morning in Sechelt and was only available at the Health Centre in the afternoons, our clinic was expected to provide backup coverage, for which we charged a $7,000 fee. In essence, it gave our doctors less than $3 per hour, a fact that was omitted when this arrangement was reported in the local press. Consequently, we were portrayed as opportunists who had tried to obstruct the establishment of the health centre in the first place in order to maintain a monopoly on medical services on the Sunshine Coast. Fortunately, after I explained the situation to Howard White, who was a member of the Pender Harbour Ratepayers' Association, a press release giving our side of the story was issued and published in a subsequent paper.[47]

Although many patients from Pender Harbour and Egmont continued to come to Sechelt for medical care, the majority of people from those communities gradually shifted to their own clinic, which has since been expanded and equipped with a small lab and an x-ray machine, a rather dubious investment since the x-rays still have to be brought to St. Mary's Hospital to be read by a radiologist. However, it has meant that the local people don't have to travel to Sechelt for x-rays.

Bonnie continued to be involved in community projects, which included a group that sponsored and looked after two families of Vietnamese refugees who came to Sechelt. Then in 1980 she was approached by her friend Evva Allen to become a partner in a jeans-and-t-shirt shop to be called the Cactus Flower. Intrigued by the idea, Bonnie agreed, even though it had been so many years since either of them had been involved in the retail business that they both needed to be taught how to use the cash register. While they shared the buying trips and took four-month shifts at looking after the books, Bonnie also worked part-time in the store and created the window displays.

In November 1983 our whole family went to see my mother at the Vancouver General Hospital where she was recovering from a difficult operation. From the diagnosis, I knew she only had a year of life remaining, and it would not be an easy time for her. That day each of us talked with her and held her hand. When we left, somewhat subdued, we managed to fit into the waiting elevator, but when we attempted to close the door, it wouldn't budge. We waited and waited and had just decided to take another elevator when one of the nurses came rushing out to tell us that Mother had taken a turn for the worse. We returned to the room and crowded around her as she breathed her last. An autopsy revealed that she died as a result of a pulmonary embolus, but it didn't explain why the elevator had malfunctioned at that exact moment. My simple Mennonite faith provided me with that answer.

As the 1980s continued, our children began to leave the nest. Karin had always wanted to be an Anglican priest, but she became involved with another Christian group while attending Simon Fraser University and eventually graduated in women's studies. After working for the RCMP in Vancouver, she moved to Kansas where she undertook religious studies and received a Bachelor of Theology degree.

Carla was the only one of my children to follow me into medicine. During her internship she often visited us in Sechelt, along with her fiance, Jack Bryson, who was a fourth-year medical student. On one of these visits they came to the hospital to assist me with an emergency surgery. Our anaesthetist, who was relatively new to Sechelt, had brought along her own boyfriend, a doctor from Europe who was working as a neonatal anaesthetist at a large tertiary care hospital in Vancouver. His experience in that ivory-tower academic centre had not prepared him for life in a rural hospital although he had begun to hear tales of some of our adventures. Towards the end of the operation I noticed him standing at the sink in the scrub room, looking through the window into the operating room. Since the surgery was essentially done, I left the closure for my assistants to do and joined him at the sink. As we washed up, he asked me what we had just done and I explained that I had dealt with a bowel obstruction. Then he asked me who was closing. Without thinking of the ramifications, I answered casually, "Oh, that's just my daughter and her boyfriend." As I saw his eyes open wide, his jaw drop a bit and an incredulous expression creep over his face, I realized how this must have sounded. However, I did not elaborate. Some months later when he knew us better, he laughed and explained that he had assumed that things were more desperate in country surgery than he had imagined, and that family members might indeed be routinely conscripted as O.R. assistants.

After their marriage Carla and Jack settled down in Sechelt. When their first baby was due, Carla tried to have a natural childbirth, but after forty-eight hours of labour it became obvious that this wasn't possible. Remembering how, when she and her siblings were young and couldn't do something, I used to infuriate them by saying, "Well, if you can't do it, I can," Carla now turned to me and said, "Well, Dad, I can't do this, so you're going to have to." Without hesitation I donned mask and gown and assisted my colleague, Rand Rudland, to do the Caesarean section, and that's how I met my grandson, Malcolm.

Guy became a database manager with the BC Arthritis Society in Vancouver. Mark stayed home for a year after he graduated from high school, then he went on to university where he earned a doctorate in physics and now teaches at Thompson Rivers University in Kamloops. After earning an arts degree in psychology from Concordia University, David became an actor, working in both television and movies.

Meanwhile, as the only surgeon on the Sunshine Coast, I continued to be on call every single hour of every single day, and the only time I could get away from this pressure was to leave the Coast. Although I had always accepted that this was part of being a country surgeon, by 1990 the regime was beginning to wear on me, and I decided that it was time for a change. Fortunately, I found a doctor who was facing the same situation. A wee bit older than me, Pat Cullum was the solo surgeon in Williams Lake. When I contacted him to ask if he would be interested in sharing a practice in Sechelt, he thought about it for a while then said, "Yeah! I'll go for that."

Our arrangement was that we would each do a rotation of four months on and four months off, and it worked so well for both of us that when Pat finally retired several years later, I found another surgeon, Andrew Piers, who was willing to continue the rotation. In this way I was able to catch my breath and gain a new perspective on life, travelling to new places with Bonnie, doing locums in communities such as Whitehorse and embarking on new and often challenging adventures.

CHAPTER 9

Itchy Feet

As chief of surgery when St. Mary's Hospital was first accredited in 1974, I had been interviewed by the Accreditation Canada surveyor, and at the end of our discussion I asked, "How did you get a job like this?"

"I had an interest in this kind of thing," he said, "going around and surveying hospitals, being an educator and facilitator. So I applied." Then, appreciating my interest, he added, "I think you'd be a good surveyor. Why don't you apply?"

Sixteen years later and with four months at my disposal, I was finally able to follow his suggestion. I was immediately accepted into the program, and after attending a three-day training session in Ottawa, I was posted to Prince Albert, Saskatchewan, as an observational surveyor. My task there was to learn from the senior surveyor and contribute my own observations. After that assignment was complete, I was a fully fledged surveyor, a position I maintained with Accreditation Canada for the next fourteen years.

In order to remain in good standing with that organization, I had to spend two weeks a year doing hospital surveys. When I first started, I would survey two a week, but as regional hospitals became the norm, I only did one a week because these evaluations would cover all of the health services in the region, which meant that the team had to examine everything the hospital or health district was doing to see if they met the national standards. If they didn't, we would make a recommendation on how they could improve. Most of the hospitals were relatively small, the largest being about two hundred beds, and I became adept at making these recommendations in a sensitive way that encouraged the hospital leaders to make the changes that were needed. Often I would discover unique and interesting procedures, and I'd bring so many of these ideas home that our director of nursing, Wendy Hunt, would greet me after each survey with, "What have you brought us? What can we do here?"

Although Accreditation Canada paid the expenses of its surveyors, the honorarium they initially provided didn't even cover the overhead on our practices back home. However, I was not doing it for the money but for the opportunity to travel into hospitals across Canada. While many of my surveys were in the Maritimes, I was also able to go to places such as Cambridge Bay, Iqaluit and Inuvik, which I would never have got to under normal circumstances. Best of all, for just the cost of her flight, Bonnie was allowed to come along and be a tourist on these adventures.

Life seemed particularly good to me during these years. When I wasn't doing surveys or travelling with Bonnie, I was spending time in the northern territories as a locum in Whitehorse or at home working in my garden or with my birds. Reflecting on my satisfaction with how things were going, I was reminded of a conversation I'd once had with my father about how I had succeeded in my professional career and how well my life had turned out. At that time he had said, "Well, there's got to be payback. A lot has been good for you, and now you've got to give back." Of course, by "giving back" my dad meant missionary work. So in 1993, with his words still ringing in my ears and lured by the prospect of yet another adventure, I contacted the International Medical Corps (IMC) in Los Angeles, and before I knew it I had signed up for a five-week posting to Somalia.

Although the IMC paid for all travel and living expenses, there would be no wages, and medical professionals were asked to bring as many supplies as they could round up. When our Hospital Employees Union heard what I was going to do, they immediately set up an account at the Bank of Montreal and within three weeks had raised $25,000. Since the pharmaceutical companies would sell to me at cost, I was able to parlay these funds into about $50,000 worth of medicines, dressings and other medical paraphernalia. At the same time the administrators at St. Mary's let me go into the supply room and load up on other things I needed. When I finally left, I had assembled about thirty boxes filled with supplies, which IMC air-freighted from Vancouver to Somalia.

In March armed with a hockey bag that Bonnie had filled with child and adult-sized t-shirts, which I was to distribute among the patients, I boarded an Air Canada plane in Vancouver, bound for London. When I told the stewardess that I was going to Somalia to volunteer my services, she wanted to move me to first class but airline rules would not allow this. Instead, the pilot invited me to sit in the cockpit for the last thirty minutes. In London I connected with a flight to Nairobi, and it was after I landed there that things began to get interesting. The Kenyan customs agents all sat at desks about four feet higher than us travellers, which was a bit intimidating, and since the Kenyans did not like the Somalis, the fact that I was bringing in thirty cases of relief supplies did not sit well with them. They did not make me feel welcome and I remained uneasy until I boarded a relief plane to Somalia. A short time later we landed in Beledweyne, a city near the Ethiopian border, three hundred kilometres north of Mogadishu.

Less than one-tenth the size of Canada, Somalia in 1993 had a population of just over seven million people, mostly Sunni Muslims who were divided into numerous clans, all claiming to descend from a common ancestor. Each main clan is composed of many subclans, among which are numerous rivalries, especially between those of the northern and southern areas. Added to this mix is a sizeable Bantu population, a people looked down upon by the Somalis.[48]

After achieving independence from Italy and Britain in 1960, the northern and southern parts of the country had joined to form the Somali Republic. However, clan rivalries, a prolonged war with Kenya, and discord with Ethiopia hindered the establishment of a stable government. In a 1969 military coup Major General Mohamed Siad Barre came to power, introducing a kind of scientific socialism to the country and allying his government with the Soviet Union, which provided arms and training for the Somali army and strengthened the country's defences against Ethiopia. The Soviet Union switched sides in 1977, forcing Barre to seek support from the United States, which eventually took over some of the abandoned Soviet bases. When Barre's popularity began to wane, his army's crackdown on dissenters grew harsher, and much of their anger was directed towards the United States.[49]

Oddly enough, one of the greatest problems in Somalia arose out of the distribution of food donated by foreign aid groups. It was intended to relieve the starvation caused by the war and recent droughts, but local leaders artificially inflated the number of people requiring aid. Most of the extra food obtained in this way was stolen and sold for profit, forcing local farmers and distributors out of business and thus inadvertently destroyed the country's agrarian-based economy. Meanwhile, Barre's atrocities caused the United States to cut off this aid, and as a result opposition to the leader increased and in January 1991 Barre's military government collapsed. A civil war ensued led by war lords who further exploited the resources of the country to finance their private armies, and the conflict disrupted the transport of food to the drought-stricken southern regions. However, by 1993 the United Nations was sending peacekeeping forces to the country, while a military coalition was effectively dealing with food distribution and creating an uneasy truce among the warring clans.[50] As a participant in the peacekeeping force, Canada had a base in Beledweyne, close to the IMC unit.

I didn't fully appreciate the history or the nature of this small country when I first arrived, and although I knew it was much, much hotter than Sechelt, I wasn't prepared for the forty-five-degree heat that hit me when I stepped off the plane in Beledweyne. *Thump!* It was just like a furnace blasting me. Nor was I prepared for the four IMC guards armed with AK47s, who met me at the airport and escorted me to a Jeep bearing the flag of the International Medical Corps. A machine gun was mounted on the vehicle's bonnet. For a while we followed the Shebelle River, a brown and unbelievably filthy waterway, which snaked through the town, and from the Jeep I could see dead animals floating slowly downstream past people who were swimming and washing clothes along the banks. In the air was the constant smell of burning charcoal caused by the small, open cooking fires that were mainly fuelled by a type of charcoal briquette. To get firewood, the people would have to go miles into the country, and they would come back with a bundle on their backs or on their donkeys' backs.

After a while we pulled up in front of the IMC compound, a villa that was once owned by a wealthy Ethiopian. As we drove through big iron gates I could see that the buildings of the compound formed a sturdy perimeter, along with the seven-foot high cement walls that were topped with barbed wire and broken glass. The guards' quarters were located right beside the gate, while mine were located in one of several single-storey buildings that faced the centre of the compound, which was an open, park-like area. My room was backed by a two-foot thick rock wall, with one tiny window that looked out onto the street. It was not big enough for a man to get through, but once when I left some of my things on the ledge, they were stolen within two days.

Among the other buildings in the compound was a cook-house where our meals were prepared and served by a Somali chef who shared his kitchen area with huge rats that could be seen scurrying everywhere. We didn't eat off the local economy since there were too many problems with bacterial infections and parasites, such as bilharzia, which can penetrate the skin of persons swimming, bathing or washing in contaminated water.[51] Instead, our food and bottled water were flown in every four or five days by the relief agency and stored in a fridge that was powered by a generator. For the first few days after each delivery we would eat fresh fish, meat and vegetables and drink beer and Coke, but after that the quality of our meals was not great. The only local food we ate was fresh fruit that could be peeled, such as grapefruit and oranges.

My small bedroom was so hot at night that I slept outside in a hammock, and in the morning I woke with the rising sun and the chirps, whistles and screech of birds. Since Beledweyne is situated right near the equator, the sun rises at six a.m. and sets at six p.m. all year round, and it constantly amazed me how these birds would start to sing at exactly the same moment that the sun peeped over the horizon. Once roused, I would head for the shower enclosure and douse myself with cool water. This luxury was made possible by a delivery boy who would come every day leading a donkey with a bell around its neck and a water barrel strapped to its back. The boy carried the water up to a large tank on a platform that was higher than our dwellings, and from there it was gravity-fed to our showers. Whenever I was working in the compound, I would go, fully clothed, into the shelter, pull the cord and let the cold water run over me for ten seconds. Then I'd walk out and as the water evaporated, it cooled me. I also discovered that my loose-fitting surgical scrubs provided the greatest relief from the heat, so I wore these all the time.

Despite the presence of UN peacekeepers, Somalia was still a pretty hostile country, and whenever I left the compound I was accompanied by some of the guards and an interpreter in the gun-mounted Jeep. Even though we flew an International Medical Corps flag on the Jeep, people looked at us with angry suspicion, and I always had the feeling that they wanted our money but not us. At night I could hear shooting beyond our compound and in the morning I would be told about the bad things that had happened. In one incident two of our public health nurses, who had gone out into the countryside to teach people how to look after their water, were shot and killed. I tried to convince myself that I was safe, but I was never sure whether our guards would protect me in a crisis, although they were paid a lot of money to do so. There were always six or eight of them sitting outside of their quarters every morning waiting to escort aid workers, and to encourage them to be on my side, whenever I passed by, I would toss them a couple of packs of cigarettes and tell them to have a good day.

Soon after my arrival, the precariousness of my position was brought home to me by my boss. In order to keep fit, I would go once a day to jog on an airfield that was controlled by the Canadian military. It was on a little plateau, and since the only planes landing there were relief and military transports, the runway was usually deserted. When my boss found out what I'd been doing, she tore a strip off me.

"You could get killed there!" she fumed. "They do that. They see you running there and someone is going to take a pot shot at you."

"I didn't realize it was that dangerous," I apologized, but she hadn't finished.

"All you do is think of yourself," she went on. "I don't need the complications your death would cause me!"

As hard as it was to get used to the physical dangers of the mission, it was harder still for me to cope with the frustration of going to the hospital and being unable to use my skills to help the people who needed them. Located one mile from our compound, the hospital was a cool brick and stucco building with about one hundred beds, a single big operating room and very old equipment. Built by the Italians in the 1930s, this medical centre was located within a secure compound that was similar to our living quarters. There was no heating required, and electricity was provided by an oil-fired plant with fuel supplied by the Canadian Airborne Division. However, much of this fuel was pilfered by the administrator until he was finally told that a tank would have to last one week. When we ran out in five days, he asked for more but was turned down, so we had no power for two days.

The hospital wards were always in a state of flux as patients slept on the floor or outside, and sometimes a sick mom and a sick baby shared the same bed. The rule was, if they brought a mattress, they could stay. The very large staff, paid by the IMC, were a lazy group, uninterested in helping, especially if their patient was from the wrong tribe. There were even times when they refused to give these patients their medications. Often when I came into a room, the nurses would be sitting on a bed, painting their hands and feet and gossiping and wouldn't even bother to make rounds with me.

I did save individual lives. I was allowed to operate on men, especially war lords and their gang members who had been shot, stabbed or blown up. Operating on their women and children, however, was a different story because that required that a surgical consent form be endorsed by the male head of the family (usually by a thumb print). The form simply stated that the patient understood that the outcome of the surgery was the will of Allah, but the women had no say in making the decision to sign it, and children even less, and by and large, the men would not give permission. In many cases I knew these little kids were going to die unless I could operate on them, and yet I wasn't allowed to do so. I would examine them and arrange for the surgery, but before it happened, they would be taken home. "It is the will of Allah," the men said.

"Why do they even come here?" I asked my interpreter one day. "Why do they waste our time?"

"I don't know, Dr. Eric," he said. "I don't know."

The work was even more disheartening for our female aid workers. A female surgeon who had served ahead of me wasn't allowed to work at all, and our nurses, most of whom had been around the world doing relief work, said Somalia was the worst place they'd ever worked because the Somalis considered them to be whores since they weren't circumcised. Even the medical people had this attitude. If a nurse gave a lecture on the topic of electrolyte imbalance in kids, for example, no one would attend. She would have to give the information to me to deliver if she wanted anyone to listen.

One of the Somali doctors had a beautiful two-year-old daughter, and one day I asked, "Abas, are you really going to circumcise your little girl when she gets to be eight?"

"Well, Dr. Eric," he said, "it's up to her mother and grandmother. They make that decision. It is a cultural thing. The man has nothing to do with it."

I said, "But you're a doctor! You know how terrible this whole thing is."

"Yes, I know," he responded. "But it is still six years away. If it happens, I will do it myself. I'll just put some freezing in and make a little nick. I won't let the traditional medicine man do it because they'll just use a sharp knife or a piece of tin from a can."

The truth is that the girls demand this procedure when they get to be eight years old because they know it's traditional and all of their friends have been done. Still, I'm not sure that they don't change their minds while they're having it done because the procedure is screamingly painful and they're held down by the grandmother and mother. However, if a girl doesn't get it done, she'll be considered a whore.

Of course, the infection rate from these circumcisions was high. The girls would be brought to me dying of fever from tetanus because after the circumcision the medicine man would pack cobwebs into the vagina to stop the bleeding and sew it up tight. I'd tell the parents, "I have got to open it up and clean the area or she will die."

"No, it's the will of Allah," the father would say, and he'd take the girl home again.

Another clan rule was that they would not accept someone with a colostomy. The first and only time I attempted to perform this surgery, my Somali doctor assistant said, "You can't do this, Dr. Eric. The family will kill you!" In my books this was a true contraindication, and needless to say, I cancelled the operation.

During the course of my stay in Somalia I acquired three shadows. One was an elderly janitor who was allowed to eat

Despite the presence of UN peacekeepers during my 1993 stint with the International Medical Corp, Somalia was still a hostile country. Relief work took place inside a secure compound with very old and limited equipment, and I was often frustrated by being unable to use my skills to help the people who needed them.

and sleep at the hospital. He was dressed in rags and wasn't paid, but he pushed a broom aimlessly all day and followed me everywhere. Feeling sorry for him, I gave him three of the short-sleeved t-shirts Bonnie had packed for me. He wore all three at the same time because he had no place to leave any personal belongings. My second shadow was a handsome young man with both hands cut off—his punishment for having offended someone. He, too, lived in the hospital complex where the nurses fed him and did his toilet. I was kind to him and from that moment on he latched onto me. The traditional medicine man was my third shadow. This elusive person came at night and undid my work. If I had set a broken bone, he would reset the break in the traditional way. My interpreter said that the patients feared and respected him more than me. For a long time he avoided me, but one day I spotted him, and hoping to put an end to his "repairs," I addressed him as "colleague." He beamed at the title, and after we had talked and exchanged medical books, he joined my small group of followers.

Besides not allowing us to do our jobs, the local crooks constantly stole from us. The medical supplies I'd brought had been stored in a warehouse in Mogadishu and were stolen when thieves broke in and took nearly a million dollars worth of supplies.

There were, however, lighter moments in my tour of duty in Somalia. One was in the children's ward at the hospital where I had distributed the t-shirts from my hockey bag. When I walked in the next day, every kid was wearing a brightly-coloured shirt with "Canada" or "Vancouver" or "Mounties" on it, and the kids were all beaming. It felt good as well to witness the efforts of the Canadian Military Airborne Division to help us and the local people. Often they would come over to our compound with K-Rations, which relieved the monotony of our own food, especially when we were waiting for a fresh delivery, and they provided fuel for our generator. They also built a bridge across the Shebelle River and outfitted a fifty-man police force, not with guns, but with smart uniforms and billy sticks. The school the Canadian soldiers built here was the first to function in Somalia in two years. They were highly respected by all of the Somalis we met. "Canadian soldiers treat us like equals," they said.

On Sundays these soldiers would come to take me to their compound for the day, to feed me and have a nice visit. Our transport on these occasions was an armoured personnel carrier in which we drove through the heart of this decrepit city. One Sunday, several Somali youths leapt onto the back of the carrier and stole three jerry cans of gas.

When I told the driver and his buddy what was happening, they responded gleefully, "Good!" Then they explained that, having experienced such thefts before, they had doctored the gas in the cans by adding sugar to it, which would effectively ruin any engine!

Yet another satisfying moment was when I played cupid with a couple who might otherwise have been forever separated by their traditions. A Bantu doctor, with whom I had become friends and occasionally brought to our compound to eat with us, and our beautiful maid, a Bantu woman from another tribe, were infatuated with each other, but their tribal customs would not allow them to talk to each other. I sat them down together, and after explaining that this was how it was done in Canada, I told them they were well suited to each other and that they should start off by talking and holding hands. It worked.

Another pleasant event occurred near the end of my tour. While having a cup of tea between cases, the door opened, and in walked a military officer, an adjutant, and two soldiers with automatic rifles. The officer asked if I was Dr. Paetkau. He then told me he was Major Brian Sadler, and was in charge of the military air traffic in that part of Africa. He went on to say that I had operated on his mother in Gibsons, BC, and she had instructed him to look me up to see if I needed anything.

I explained that a relief plane would be coming for me in the early morning of my last day, but if it was possible to leave later in the day, it would allow for more surgeries. The major instructed his adjutant to make this arrangement and he grinned as he said that I had probably never had a military major as my travel agent before!

But the lighter moments didn't make up for the heart-breaking frustration and I wasn't sorry to leave this dusty, war-torn country of brutal extremes. Even the long flight home was bearable, and when I arrived back on the Sunshine Coast, I told Bonnie, "If I ever complain about the ferry service again, just say the word 'Somalia' to me!"

Of course, the Sunshine Coast has its own tragedies. I had to deal with the violent death of an attractive twenty-one-year-old woman, the victim of a car accident in which the driver had been drinking heavily. As usual, a coroner's jury was required, only this time the police called all of the local young fellows who were known to do a lot of drinking and driving and told them they had each been randomly selected for jury duty. Adhering to the custom in these cases, the jury met at John Harvey's Funeral Home. I had done the autopsy and covered the grossly mutilated body with a white sheet. With a fair degree of bravado, the young jurists positioned themselves around the table to identify the body and ask salient questions. When I ripped off the sheet in a single motion, every one of them staggered back as though hit by a sledge hammer. It was a brutal tactic, but it shook them up enough to take a second look at their own lives, and at least two of them settled down and have since become successful businessmen.

It was good, however, to be back in a community where I had a personal connection with so many families. This was made clear to me late one night as I was driving home from the ferry and picked up two young hitchhikers. I recognized one of the boys because many years earlier I had been his mother's doctor and had delivered four of her children. On the last occasion, when I told her that she had given birth to another boy, she asked if I minded if she named him after me. Now, as we drove along, I inquired about his mother and each of his brothers, identifying them by name, and I could tell by his expression that he was frantically trying to figure out who I was. Since I was going to the hospital anyway, I dropped the boys off at the Reserve and it was at this point that he blurted out, "Are you a cop?" He had been in a lot of trouble with the law, and he just assumed that was why I knew him. He was much relieved when I told him who I was.

Change is a constant on the Sunshine Coast and the medical staff at our clinic had undergone many transformations over the years as new doctors joined our practice and others left, and by that time the only one who had been there as long as I had was Walter Burtnick. During one of his sabbaticals Walter had studied surgery in orthopaedics at Bath, England, where he had developed good surgical techniques and consequently he could do a lot of procedures. He was such a strong, gentle man that he was always comfortable to be around and loved by both his patients and our staff at the clinic. But in 1993, he decided to branch out on his own, and although we remained good friends and he still participated in our Friday lunches at the Wakefield, I missed having him at the clinic.

Not that I was spending much time there myself since I was continuing with my four-month rotations, and soon after Walter opened his new office, I was making preparations for my second medical mission, an adventure that was initiated by local mining entrepreneur Reg Davis. Having made a lot of money in mining ventures in Canada, he was now trying to obtain a concession on a gold mine in Tajikistan. Faced with stiff competition from Italian, German and French mining companies, he decided it might help his chances if he were to make a substantial donation of money and medical equipment to the

Denis Rogers, doctor, adventurer, friend, before our trip to Tajikistan.

government of Tajikistan and also to send a couple of doctors over there to help out. He approached Denis Rogers with the plan, who in turn approached me, and in the end the two of us agreed to go.

After training as a navigator in the RCAF followed by a posting to Newfoundland, Denis had gone to medical school in Belfast before making his way to our clinic in 1972. Besides being colleagues, we had become close friends and did a lot of hiking and biking together, so there was no question of us being compatible on this mission. This time neither of us was interested in mounting a major campaign for funds, but we did pack a few medical supplies, and after being told that it would be smart to take along pantyhose and lipstick for the nurses, we gathered up as many of those items as possible. In this I was helped by the local Pharmasave, where Denis's wife Agatha worked, and they donated hundreds of sample tubes of lipstick. Finally in early October 1994 I left to visit with friends in Germany and a week later Denis met me in Frankfurt where we boarded a Lufthansa plane that flew to Tashkent, Uzbekistan.

Tajikistan is a republic in central Asia bordered by Uzbekistan, Kirghizstan, Afghanistan and China. The country gained independence from Russia in 1991, shortly after the collapse of the Soviet Union. The following summer civil war broke out between rival ethnic groups, which resulted in over 20,000 casualties and hundreds of thousands of refugees, but because a ceasefire had been called just a month before we were to arrive, we were assured that there was no actual shoot-ing going on.[52]

Our base was in Khujand (known as Leninabad during the Soviet era), which had a population of just over 164,000 people and was the second-largest city in Tajikistan.[53] Founded by Alexander the Great and located in the northern Fergana Valley, the city is isolated by the Turkestan and Zeravshan mountains and nourished by the Syr Darya River, which winds through Khujand on its way to nearby Uzbekistan. When we saw it, this river was only a trickle compared to its former grandeur, the result of the Soviet's "central planning" for the area, which decreed that only cotton would be grown in the valley. Since this crop requires a lot of water, the river was dammed for irrigation, a strategy that ultimately contributed to the Aral Sea drying up.[54] Goats, which were introduced around the same time, defoliated everything they could reach, leaving the riverbanks barren. But apparently the Soviets had not been the first to alter the environment of Khujand; we were told that Genghis Khan had deforested this region to cultivate grass for his livestock.

Since it was October, the city's fruit, nut, plane and other deciduous trees were all in splendid fall colours that were off-set by darker evergreens. There were no gardens visible, and the boulevards we saw were a mess, even on the university campus. The only beautiful grounds were at the new modern Levi jeans factory, and this area was fenced in.

Soon after our arrival, Denis and I realized that even if there was no open warfare, the country was still in a state of turmoil and uncertainty. The older members of the population had been hit especially hard for they had grown accustomed to having housing, health care and food provided for them by the state, and now suddenly they had nothing. While many of these people had somehow managed to sequester a lot of money dur-ing those years, rising inflation was rapidly eating into their savings. Although some things were incredibly cheap, such as a subway fare, which was the equivalent of a penny, and rent, which was fifty cents a month, other necessities, including petrol, medicine and food, were incredibly expensive. A Mars bar, for example, cost $3 US! We didn't buy many but once when we did, I remarked, "Denis, this would pay six months' rent for somebody here!"

There was also no money to maintain the city's infrastructure or to upgrade the hydro-electric and water systems. Except for hospitals and other priority institutions, gas and electricity were rationed. In most houses water was provided for just three to six hours a day and even then it was not safe to drink. Community toilets were plugged up, there were no lights in the restrooms and no money to pay for cleaning them, so people would just do their toilet outside on the riverbank, which meant we had to be very careful where we walked.

Our living quarters in Khujand were along that riverbank in a two-storey building that had once been a rehabilitation centre. Under Soviet rule a person who had suffered a heart attack would be sent to such a centre for three months where, except for daily walks, he was advised to rest a lot. If the patient was a man, his whole family moved into one of the building's apartments so the wife could look after him. Now that medical services were no longer free, such a facility was too expensive for most people and it was being used instead to house hospital staff. The apartment that Denis and I were allotted was rustic, but it had a bathroom and two bedrooms, and we didn't need anything else. We did note with some amusement that the people who came to clean, make up our beds and do our laundry also used our toilet because we had brought along our own soft toilet paper, a luxury they didn't have.

Although we visited other regional hospitals, our main work was done in Khujand in a hospital that was not only short of equipment but also of basic supplies such as gloves and dressings. I discovered this the first time I made rounds. I wanted to look at a patient's wound, so I took the dressing off and threw it in the garbage as I would in Sechelt. When I finished my examination, I told the nurses that they could now put on a new dressing. Instead they retrieved the old one from the garbage, cleaned it up and put it back on! Their response to my objection was simple: they had nothing else.

Denis and I had brought a lot of equipment and some supplies, such as sutures, needles and about one hundred disposable scalpels, the kind that are intended to be used once and then discarded. About three weeks into my tour, while operating on my second case of the day, I thought I recognized a small nick in my scalpel handle.

"Is this the same scalpel I used in the previous case?" I asked the nurse.

She replied, "Doctor, that's the same scalpel you have used since you got here!"

The doctors in Tajikistan often received no pay at all, and when they *were* compensated, the wages were usually less than $18 a month. One obstetrician we befriended received ten cents for a delivery! Yet despite their poverty and difficult working conditions, both the doctors and the rest of the staff were friendly, eager to please and learn and always very concerned about our welfare and safety. On most mornings, one of the doctor's wives would get up early and prepare a hot breakfast for us, which her husband would deliver. There were always lots of leftovers for us and for the stray cats that lived in and around our apartment. At lunchtime food appeared in the doctor's lounge, and at dinner, if we weren't invited out for a feast at some doctor's house, we ate leftovers or shopped for food.

One of the places we shopped at was the Panchshanbe Bazaar, a place so huge that I don't think you could walk across it in a day. Here we found everything imaginable for sale— electrical appliances, knives of all descriptions, food and every kind of animal, including "ramsbottom," a very sturdy ram with enormous testicles hanging almost to the ground. It was the custom to bargain for everything at the market. Although I was sure we could have passed for Russians, the people seemed to know instinctively that we were foreigners, and many of the hucksters tried very aggressively to trade their goods for Yankee dollars, which was illegal. When the market was especially crowded, I did worry but our doctor friends were always nearby looking out for us.

The doctors also used their precious resources, including a twelve-passenger van they had at their disposal, to show us around their country. The vehicle was a bit of a wreck, but it enabled them to take us on a trip to Samarkand in neighbouring Uzbekistan. There were fourteen of us in the van, including a friend of one of the doctors who just happened to be the city's chief of police. At first the road we were travelling was paved, and I was able to relax and enjoy the countryside streaming past—small farms with remnants of the fall harvest lingering in the fields, occasionally a grove of trees dressed in robes of gold and orange, and always the mountains to which we were drawing ever closer. Then suddenly our driver

Denis Rogers, our host doctor, Maxmuda, and I stand in front of a wall built by Alexander the Great—still in decent shape!

slowed, and looking ahead we could see a barricade across the highway where a group of soldiers stood with machine guns pointed right at us. Everyone was silent as the van crept slowly forward under the scrutiny of the soldiers, until we were close enough for them to see the police chief, who was sitting in the front seat. At once the head soldier stepped back, saluted and waved us through.

Recovering my voice, I asked the chief, "Who are they and what are they doing here?"

"Well," he said, "that's our military."

"What were they checking for?"

"Fundamentalists from Afghanistan who are infiltrating this country," he responded. "They try to smuggle guns into this country and cause problems."

"And what," I dared, "would they have done if they had found a fundamentalist in our van?"

His answer was brief. "Shoot him."

I fell silent, digesting this information then turned my attention back to the mountainous terrain we were now travelling through.

Shortly after lunchtime we arrived at a farm that had been an experimental agricultural station under the Soviets. We were introduced to the owner and his extended family, and then Denis and I were taken by one of the men, who spoke no English, to a sheep paddock. The man smiled as he showed us his flock, and as we nodded and tried to convey by our smiles how nice everything looked, he picked up one of the sheep and held it out to us. Again we smiled and nodded. "Yeah, yeah, nice sheep." As soon as he could see that we liked the sheep, the man pulled a butcher knife from a holder on his belt and promptly slit the animal's throat right in front of us! That's when we realized that he wanted our approval of the animal because we were going to eat him. I felt so bad that we had inadvertently done in this poor little sheep that I had difficulty eating the feast that was prepared especially for us—fruit and nuts, soup, a rice pilaf with shredded lamb, and, of course, the ever-present vodka.

On another trip we drove along the M34 through the Shakhristan Pass, a rugged route with breathtaking views of the snow-capped peaks of the Turkestan range. At the top of the pass we blew a tire, and it was then that Denis and I noticed that all of the tires were bald. Of the two spares, only one was useable and it, too, was in bad shape, and we realized that if we had another flat, we would be stranded. Fortunately we made it to the small city of Penzekant intact, and there we spent the night. When our fellow passengers were not around, Denis and I gave our interpreter the money to buy two decent tires on the black market but requested that he keep our contribution a secret from those very proud people.

Once I was presented with a very complex case—a thirty-year-old woman with crescending thyroiditis (also called Hashimoto's disease), a condition in which the immune system attacks the thyroid gland. Untreated it could become life-threatening. It was too much for us to handle with the limited resources of the hospital in Khujand, but her brother, who was very rich, offered to drive us in his new Mitsubishi sedan to the medical centre at the University of Tashkent in Uzbekistan, four hours away. There I met the professor of surgery and discussed the case, but he couldn't help. With tears in his eyes, he told me they had nothing, not even sterile gloves. So I took her back to Khujand. I tried to stir up some interest with surgeons I knew in Vancouver, but the issues involved in bringing her to Canada for surgery were just too complex. Then I suggested to her brother that he fly her to the States. I never saw her again, so I don't know whether he followed my advice or not.

At the end of our tour, it was pretty plain to Denis and I that we had failed to bring these people what they really needed. While our gifts of lipstick and pantyhose were a hit with the nurses in the five regional hospitals we visited, they were no substitute for the dressings and other supplies that would have

The fall of communism had turned the Tajikistan economy topsy-turvy. Rents were still fifty cents a month, and doctors often received little or no pay. This obstetrician (at right) received seven cents per delivery. Denis Rogers is seated in the middle.

helped to save lives. Before flying home, I spent three nights in Tashkent, staying in an old Soviet-style building called the Hotel Uzbekistan, where they had never heard of credit cards. Rooms were paid for in cash, one day at a time, and each floor was guarded by a big lady in a uniform who would collect the receipt then give out a room key. Whenever I left, the woman on my floor would take my key back, eyeing me suspiciously as if she was worried that I might be stealing something from the room. One evening I used the manager's office to telephone Bonnie and was charged $10 a minute for the call.

The first morning after my arrival I was standing in the lobby of the hotel and wondering how I would spend the day when a young man approached and in perfect English introduced himself as Igor and asked if he could be my guide for the day. Although his usual charge was $7, I said if he gave me a great tour I would pay $10. After a thoroughly satisfying day we came to a square with an opera house where one of my favourites, *La Traviata*, was being staged. Igor said that he had never been to an opera, so I told him to go to the kiosk where people were already lining up and purchase two of the best seats available. He came back empty-handed to tell me that the best seats cost twice as much as regular seats.

"Get them anyway," I said. This time he returned to say that the salesperson, having heard my conversation with Igor, had determined that I was an American and was making special arrangements for us. They then proceeded to kick two people from their seats in the front row and give them to me as an "honoured guest!" Igor loved the opera so much he was crying at the end and planned to go again one day.

That night I went into the hotel restaurant for a late dinner. The enormous dining room was empty except for one long table where about twenty-four men were seated. When the waiter ushered me to a seat at the end of the table I figured it was just another example of Uzbekistan's efficiency. Then the man next to me began talking in English, and I discovered they

Although the country was still in a state of turmoil and uncertainty, Tajikis were very hospitable, sharing what little they had with us. Everywhere we went, we were shown such generosity.

were all part of an American air squadron that had been invited to do some surveillance work for the Uzbekian government.

The man sitting next to me at that dinner was the squadron's flight doctor, and he joined me for my final day of touring with Igor, this time to a huge art gallery where we both wanted to buy paintings that were priced at $400 each. Unfortunately, here, too, they did not know about credit cards, and when I showed mine to the attendant and predicted that in five years she would be accepting credit cards instead of cash, she could not believe such a thing would ever happen.

In 1997 Mack Bryson and I travelled to Nepal, stopping enroute in Bangkok to stay with my cousin, Mark. Although we were not on a medical mission, while there I was commissioned to do a mock accreditation survey at the Kings Hospital, a 5,000-bed facility that was in transition between the traditional methods practised by older doctors and the modern methods of younger doctors who had been trained in the west.

In Nepal we hiked the Annapurna Trail, starting at the lakeside city of Pokhara, 884 metres (2,900 feet) above sea level. From here we were less than thirty kilometres from Fishtail Mountain, which we could easily see along with Dhaulagiri, Manaslu and five other peaks of the Annapurna Range. Hiking into this rugged expanse that varied from steamy subtropical jungles to freezing glacial peaks seemed a daunting undertaking, but we had a private guide and a porter to show us the way, and as was my custom, I had brought a lot of medical supplies "just in case." Within three hours of starting out I had to repair the badly smashed face of a German doctor. His partner, though a nurse, was unable to help because she was in a faint. Instead, Mack became my assistant for the two-hour repair which was performed at the side of the trail while countless people trekked past us, all stopping to look. Both the doctor and his nurse companion were fine when we finished, and as we continued our trek, we found that the "surgeon and the cowboy" had become famous. At the start of each day, everyone wanted to leave ahead of us—just in case—and at the end of every day we held a clinic. Mack loved being my assistant and learned very quickly how to examine people for possible sprains.

For twelve days we travelled deeper and deeper into the mountains, sometimes following stone-paved pathways through gnarled rhododendron forests and other times picking our way along rocky ridges high above seemingly impassable canyons. We crossed sagging suspension bridges over turquoise rivers far below and trekked through green terraced rice fields and villages where mud-brick houses showed the effects of age and weather. Each day the geography and climate of the trail shifted, taking us from hot and muggy lowlands to cold, windswept highlands and snowy glaciers and from the wide gravel bed of the Kali Gandaki River to the soothing hot springs of Tatopani. After one particularly gruelling climb we came to a teahouse with a big sign that read, "Life is uncertain, eat dessert first!" It is advice that I have tried to follow ever since.

As we climbed higher and higher the air grew thinner and the landscape wilder, often resembling a moonscape, and by the time we reached Muktinath, 3,817 metres (12,523 feet) above sea level, we were getting a bit short of breath, especially at night. As it seemed foolish to push our luck and risk altitude sickness, we ended our hike at this point and boarded a Canadian-made Otter, which flew us to Kathmandu, and from there we headed home.

Two years later I travelled to Peru with Mack, Jack Bryson, and one of their friends for another high-altitude hike, this one along the Inca Trail to the ruins of Machu Picchu, 2,430 metres (8,000 feet) above sea level. For three days we trekked up paths—many lined with Incan paving stones—to ridges high above the Urubamba River, then descended into valleys only to head back up again to another pass. At night we camped near the ruins of terraced Inca villages. On June 20 we reached the ruins of Wiñawayna (Forever Young), and the following

Mack Bryson and I prepare to hold an evening clinic in a typical tea house on the Annapurna trail. As we continued our trek into the mountains, we found that "the surgeon and the cowboy" had become famous.

morning we climbed to the Sun Gate before dawn. At the portal we stood to watch the sun rise over Machu Picchu. Like everyone else who has ever witnessed this wonder, we were awed by both the breathtaking view and the sheer magnificence of what the ancient Incas had achieved.

Unfortunately, our delight was shadowed a few days later when we returned to Lima where a very officious Delta Airlines agent denied us access to our midnight flight home. We were travelling business class compliments of nurse Ingrid Turner's brother, who was a Delta pilot, and by the agent's standards were not dressed appropriately. The next morning we went shopping for proper attire and that night we tried again. This time the agent objected to Mack's ratty old duffle bag, which he had been forced to use after his suitcase was stolen earlier on the trip. Fortunately, after making us sweat for an hour, she relented and allowed us to board.

My third and final medical mission was prompted by an ad in a medical magazine I was reading one cold December day in 2000. The ad was sponsored by a non-profit group called Poco a Poco ("little by little") founded in 1995 by Dr. Jill Sampson of Qualicum Beach, BC, and it called for volunteers to provide free surgical care in Guatemala. The group organized teams of surgeons, general practitioners, anaesthetists, surgical and operating room nurses and other medical and technical personnel who would spend one to two weeks providing free surgical aid to the people of Antigua, Guatemala.[55]

Intrigued, I showed the ad to Bonnie, and after further investigation we signed on for the next aid mission, which would be leaving in February. Before that day arrived, however, much work needed to be done because not only was each participant expected to pay his own travel, accommodation and other expenses, but he was also expected to raise funds for the project and to collect a hockey bag full of medical supplies. Fortunately, since we ran our fundraising campaign over Christmas, the spirit of giving was high and we soon had everything we needed.

There were about twenty-five medical personnel in the group that came together at the Vancouver airport, including a couple of technicians who were needed to repair wheelchairs and other equipment-related emergencies that might arise during our stay. Others like Bonnie would help out wherever they could. We were a noisy bunch during our Continental Airlines flight to Houston, and we must have presented quite a picture as we disembarked, each of us lugging an enormous hockey bag along with our regular luggage. The man behind the Continental service desk wore a most bewildered expression as we trooped past.

"We're all going to a hockey tournament in Guatemala," I told him.

"Really?" he asked, looking impressed. I had no time to set

him straight because I had to catch up to the rest of my group who were hurrying to catch our connecting flight.

In Guatemala City we boarded a bus for the hour-long drive to Antigua, a mountain city surrounded by three volcanoes. Agua, less than ten kilometres away, dominates the southern skyline, while Fuego and Acatenango are more distant. Founded in 1543, Antigua was the country's capital until it was destroyed by earthquakes in 1773 and was replaced by Guatemala City. Although Antigua never regained its former glory, the rebuilt city has now been designated a world heritage site by the United Nations, which means nothing can be changed.[56] As we entered the city, the bus bumped its way along cobblestone streets bordered by narrow sidewalks and picturesque adobe buildings, most of them single-storeyed and painted in soothing pastel colours. Here and there we saw ornate churches, government buildings with colonial columns while thick-walled archways spanned the streets.

Our living quarters were in a modern complex with swimming pools and every amenity we could possibly want. We were given the rest of the day and night to rest up from our journey, and the following morning we all met at the Hermano Pedro hospital for our orientation.

Although originally built in the 1600s, the hospital had been destroyed several times by earthquakes, the last time in 1974. Reconstructed ten years later through the efforts of a Franciscan priest, the complex now covered a full city block and included an orphanage, a home for the elderly and handicapped, a nutrition and dental centre, a chapel and the 500-bed hospital.[57] With no government funding, the facility was relying on donations, and medical teams from around the world who came, as we did, to spend one or two weeks providing medical and surgical care for chronically ill people who couldn't afford to go to private facilities and didn't qualify for care at the National Hospital, which only treated acute cases.

The surgical unit had three operating rooms and

state-of-the-art equipment, some of it better than we had in Sechelt, all of it donated by visiting medical teams. The store-room that contained the surgical supplies was huge and well stocked. I thought I was being very generous with my donation of a couple of sheets of Marlex mesh along with my other con-tributions because it cost over $15 a sheet. I felt rather embar-rassed when I saw the huge cartons of the same mesh that had been donated by American teams on a previous mission.

The wide verandah fronting the surgical unit was filled with people ranging from the very old to the very young, many of whom had travelled for days just for the chance to see if we could help them or their children. Our first task after the orientation was to examine these people and assess whether an operation would help them. Unfortunately, of the more than two hundred people who waited that morning, only about fifty qualified for surgical intervention during the time we had there.

While I was busy in the operating room, Bonnie was help-ing out in the pre-op and post-op areas of the hospital, assisting the nurses and working with patients. When our day was over, we would go with the rest of our group to a local bar for a beer and then on to a nice restaurant for dinner. Bonnie and I both enjoyed walking down streets where there were no big signs. Even McDonald's was unidentifiable and unless someone told you where it was, you'd never find it. We did, however, have to be careful not to walk into the wrought iron grillwork that covered the windows of most houses and shops for they often took up most of the narrow walkway. To avoid these, many people simply walked on the street.

Unlike my previous missions, I felt safe in Guatemala and appreciated. People were eternally grateful for everything we did and everybody seemed to be smiling and friendly. When we left, we promised ourselves we would come back one day, but somehow that has never happened. We are always too busy with our other activities.

CHAPTER 10

Medicine Changes, People Don't

Life was certainly easier for us in Sechelt with my four-month-on, four-month-off rotation, but during my "on" times every community activity I participated in continued to be undermined by the fact that I might have to leave without warning for a medical emergency. I had become inured to the drama associated with these emergencies, though occasionally I still experienced the thrill of being a key player in a major event.

One afternoon while judging a high school science fair in Pender Harbour, I received a call from the operating room nurse at St. Mary's that I was needed immediately in surgery to deal with an uncontrollable hemorrhage. After a hasty explanation to the organizers of the fair, I hurried to my car and headed for Sechelt. Driving a bit faster than the speed limit, I was musing that it would be nice to have a police escort when, lo and behold, at Middlepoint I encountered a speed trap that was facing the opposite direction. I screeched to a stop, identified myself to the officer and quickly explained my problem. Although he was a Vancouver Mountie, new to the Sunshine Coast and obviously not sure what to make of me, he reluctantly agreed to be my escort, but for the first three minutes or so after we started out he drove in a sedate manner at the upper range of the speed limit. I had just decided that I had made a serious error in judgement when suddenly his lights and sirens went on and he floored it. Now he was flying ahead, far too fast for my liking, but I hung on behind him. (I found out later that, while driving at the slower speed, he had called the hospital and Julie McIntyre, the operating nurse, had told him to get me there as fast as possible.) As we sped past the four major intersections en route to the hospital, I saw that the police had barricaded all cross traffic, including the road turning into the hospital. It was an exhilarating moment as we raced past the waiting cars and swept into the parking lot. Unfortunately, it was all in vain. There was nothing anyone could do to stop the bleeding and the patient died soon after my arrival.

Exhilarating as they were, such moments only added to the constant stress of being on call twenty-four hours a day, seven days a week. Compounding this was the gradual deterioration of my ability to hear, a condition brought home to me when Ingrid Turner, one of the nurses in the operating room, remarked, "E.P., I can tell you are getting old!"

"How so?" I asked.

"Well, for one thing, you're getting deaf. And secondly, you can't control your farts!"

Of course, she was only partly accurate. Because I could no longer hear my farts, I didn't think anyone else could either.

Even more stressful were the changes that had been occurring in our local and provincial health care system over the previous twenty years.

In some ways these changes were good. For example, at one time surgeons made the decisions surrounding a patient's care, such as whether an operation would produce a better outcome than no surgery at all. In the past two decades, however, I had changed my style as a surgeon and instead of making these critical choices myself, I would present my patient with options—this is your diagnosis, and these are the alternative treatments available for this condition. You tell me what you want done. If you want to keep your gall bladder, you can keep it. If you want it out, fine. Generally, this had made my life easier, although some people still asked, "Well, what do *you* think I should do?"

With the internet and easier access to medical information, the expectations of patients had also increased. In the early days they would say, "Well, Doctor, do your best." Now if the best didn't happen, the doctor was in trouble. However, this new familiarity with medical terms could lead to humorous misunderstandings, such as happened when I was asked to consult on a lady who had a significant lesion of her umbilicus. After explaining the options, I advised her that the best treatment would be to have the umbilicus removed. There was a moment's pause, and then this forty-year-old lady smiled gently and said, "That's okay, Doctor, I don't need it. I'm not going to have any more children anyway."

There had been positive changes, too, in diagnostics and other medical advances. Where once we had to come up with a diagnosis based on the patient's history and a laying-on-of-hands, as it were, now we could do a CAT Scan or an MRI and have the medical problem confirmed instantly. There were times in the early days as well when I was called on to perform emergency surgeries that stretched the limits of my abilities. Now we had helicopters that could take these patients to specialized surgical units in the Lower Mainland.

In other areas, however, I was disturbed by the deterioration of our health care system. From 1955, when the St. Mary's Hospital Society was incorporated, until 1993 our hospital had been governed by a board of seven trustees elected by members of the community who belonged to the Society—a privilege open to anyone for the fee of $1. Also on the board was a government-appointed representative and, until 1964, a representative from the Columbia Coast Mission. The board members were business people who didn't have any experience with health care, so in those days the chief of staff—a position that Al Swan, Walter Burtnick and I alternated in for many years—went to all the meetings and had major input. We'd talk about something and they'd say, "Well, what do you think we should do, Doctor?" When we gave our answers, they listened.

In 1993 this system was changed by the NDP government, which was already waging a battle with doctors over legislated limits to their billing amounts. Suddenly all local health services, including hospitals, were managed, and funding decisions were turned over to community health councils under the umbrella of twenty regional health boards across the province. Each community health council was comprised of both elected representatives and government appointees. While most of the members had no experience in the field of health care, the majority had been involved either on previous hospital boards or in local social service organizations.[58] A doctor was still allowed to be on the council and provide some input into the decisions made, and in Sechelt I often filled this position. But because the new mandate was to base decisions on the needs of the *whole* health community, not just those of the hospital and the medical staff, we had to consider St. Mary's Hospital's services as well as three residential care facilities, home support, an adult day program, caregivers support, a home-based detox program, and volunteer services such as Meals on Wheels, volunteer drivers, a telephone tree and a hospice program.[59] Over the next eight years the twenty regional health boards were reduced to eleven for the whole province, and province-wide the number of community health councils fell from one hundred to fifty-two.

After the Social Credit party was elected in 2001, health care in British Columbia once again underwent a massive change. Community health councils were eliminated in favour of five health regions for the whole province, and the Sunshine Coast's health system, including the public health unit, was now governed by the Vancouver Coastal Health Authority. Made up of six to nine government-appointed board members and a chief executive officer, this new board is responsible for the health needs of over one million people and covers Vancouver and the Sea-To-Sky corridor communities of Whistler, Pemberton, and the Sunshine Coast, including Powell River. As with the other boards we had dealt with, none of the VCHA board members had a medical background. The big difference was that these new leaders were not about to pay much attention to what doctors said was needed, and doctors were no longer invited to attend board meetings, even though we were the ones who knew what was going on at our hospitals. Suddenly medical services were all about money, and since doctors were one of the major expenses, we were now considered adversaries instead of partners in a team.

Just ten years earlier we had one of the finest health care systems in the world, but after the system was dismantled and restructured with no input from health professionals, we hit rock bottom. For me, one of the more difficult aspects of this new order was the bureaucracy that now hindered so many of my decisions. For example, where at one time I could easily refer a patient to a specialist, now I had to go through time-consuming and often frustrating formalities.[60]

Perhaps the greatest issue facing the medical community in 2002, however, was that there were simply not enough doctors, a situation rooted in Justice Emmett Hall's 1980 report in which he raised the possibility of a physician surplus in Canada and recommended that a physician workforce study be carried out. (Surprisingly, Justice Hall had chaired a Royal Commission on Health Services in 1964, and at that time had recommended doubling the number of places for the study of medicine in Canada.)[61] The studies, dutifully undertaken by provincial governments, concluded that medical school enrolments should be reduced, much to the objections of doctors across the nation. When a 1991 report by M.L. Barer and G.L. Stoddart also recommended cuts, provincial and territorial governments were quick to comply, and between 1993 and 1999 there was a 17.3

percent decrease in undergraduate enrolment.[62] Unfortunately, these same governments failed to implement any of the other twenty-nine recommendations in the Barer-Stoddart report, such as an increase in the number of nurse-practitioners in Canada.[63] When 1999 statistics showed that this policy had resulted in physician shortages of 30.4 percent for family doctors and 36.7 percent for specialists, provincial governments started to increase enrolments, and these have been going up ever since. However, it will take a lot of years for the increases to trickle down into the field because the retirement rate is also on the rise.

Two other factors affecting the availability of physicians in Canada were the increased enrolment of women in medical schools and the changing demands of young doctors. In 1960 only 9.4 percent of medical students were women, but by 1995 this had risen to 50 percent. While these women are every bit as efficient and proficient as men, their commitment to raising children and looking after their homes means that they practice an average of 7.3 hours a week less than their male counterparts. At the same time, while doctors of my generation would stay on the job until the work was done, often remaining in the office until after seven p.m., today's young doctors are demanding forty-hour weeks. I don't blame them, but fewer doctor-hours mean that the province still has a physician shortage.

To counteract this, our governments increased their use of international medical graduates (IMGs), often allowing them to practice in Canada on the condition that they spend a certain number of years in an area where the physician shortage is critical. The hope was that these doctors would ultimately remain in these communities, but not many do. There is also the moral issue of Canada stealing good doctors from countries that need them, such as South Africa. However, when I was doing locums in the north, I discovered that many of the IMGs working there had not been trained to the same standards that we are here, and some of them were totally unqualified. Unfortunately, there are not enough residencies available in Canada for all IMGs to upgrade their skills. It is known that if medical students are recruited from rural areas, they are more likely to return to rural areas when they graduate. Those raised in cities, however, seldom want to go into the country, yet no allowance is made for these circumstances in our medical school entrance requirements. For the past few years I have interviewed prospective students for medical school, and I always ask them about their aspirations. Of course, it is well known that I have a bias towards those who want to practice in rural areas, and while I'm quite certain that many of them will never leave Vancouver, they all say, "My fondest wish is to be a country doctor!" It would work far better if there were a certain number of medical school spots left open for kids from the country, as has been the case at the University of Northern BC where I have often worked as a locum. When I talked to the kids I was teaching, I found that many of them were from the north and they were flat out enthusiastic about staying in the north.

All of these difficulties—the bureaucratic upheavals, the physician shortages and the constant pressure of being on call twenty-four hours a day—are both challenges and opportunities not unlike those the medical community was facing when I walked through the doors of the University of Saskatchewan and took my first step towards a career in medicine. Like the old challenges, these new obstacles will eventually be dealt with, though not by me.

In 2002 it was forty-two years since Bonnie and I drove along the winding gravel road to Garden Bay, searching for a country hospital perched on a small bluff overlooking the waters of Hospital Bay. In those years I had grown with our adopted community, perfecting my skills as a surgeon in an ever-changing environment, moving from the rickety operating room table that was elevated by placing bricks under the legs to a state-of-the-art surgical unit in a new hospital that was once again facing a major expansion. I felt comfortable in this

In June 2002 I officially gave up my scalpel and with thanks to all my co-workers, had the retirement party to end all retirement parties.

community and sensed that the community felt comfortable with me. In fact, one of my favourite memories is of the feeling I would get after I'd been called out in the middle of the night and done something really worthwhile. Heading home again at three in the morning, I would go down Sechelt's main street and no one was there. Driving through in the darkness, I felt like I was a kind of health guardian for the people of the Sunshine Coast.[64]

But it was time for me to pass that guardianship to younger hands, and in June 2002 I officially retired as the surgeon of the Sunshine Coast. Henceforth, my days would be spent working in my garden, spending more time with my growing number of grandchildren and visiting with friends.

Not that I went silently into the night. There were still accreditation visits to make to other hospitals and opportunities for teaching colleagues, nurses and medical students, jobs I both enjoyed and seemed to have a talent for. I also continued to do surgical locums in northern BC, Manitoba and the Yukon, and of course, here in Sechelt.

Then one night during the winter of 2010–11 as I sat in the stands at a local hockey game, I asked Dale Benner, who was sitting beside me, to tell me the names of the boys playing on the ice.

"Why?" he asked. "Because you might have delivered them?"

"No," I said, "because I might have delivered their parents."

We chuckled, but as I watched the rest of the game I thought, "It's time."

EPILOGUE

Before I Go . . .

I practised in the golden age of medicine in British Columbia when patients' expectations were lower and, "Doctor, you know best," was the patient's usual response when presented with treatment options. It was a time when physicians were more in charge, especially in small town hospitals where locally elected volunteer boards asked for and valued their doctors' opinions, and community support was enormous.

At St. Mary's I had the good fortune to work in a unique and stimulating environment. Isolated from the city by the ferry, right from day one the relationship among my colleagues was one of mutual respect and understanding, and I do not recall a single episode of unpleasantness among us. The atmosphere in the O.R., my main environment, was cheerful, friendly and harmonious, and the long-time head nurses—Natalie Gardiner, Jean Stewart and Marg MacKenzie—made my life easy. Other O.R. nurses were equally supportive—"Radar" Blanca ("Give him what he needs, not what he asks for"), Charlotte who said a silent prayer before handing me the scalpel, Ingrid who recognized and articulated the frailties of an aging surgeon, creating major outbursts of laughter, and Julie McIntyre whose voice of encouragement could always be heard in the background,

"Good work, E.P." My relationship with the rest of the hospital staff was also easygoing, pleasant and cooperative.

Of course, my career had taken a heavy toll on my family who had to endure constant disruptions to planned events, vacations that had to be taken off the Coast, and my long absences. Carla recalls that when she was a going-concern teenager that there was a period we didn't even see each other for three weeks. During these periods, Bonnie was always called on to do double duty. Still, I have this difficulty with retirement—I'm not very good at it. But a recent one/two punch has made me see the end point. The first occurred when my old friend Brenda Rowe, an O.R. nurse, saw me at the hospital and asked gently if I had lost my caregiver. A short time later Wendy Hunt, retired director of nursing, saw me and asked, "Don't you have a 'best before' date?"

My scalpel has grown heavy, the operating room curtains are closing, and somewhere out there I can hear the fat lady singing.

Postscript:

On June 23, 2011, I was in Thompson, Manitoba and awoke at midnight, Central Daylight Time, from a most vivid dream. In my dream, I was in a roomful of unknown people, and at the centre was Al Swan, in full health. With a gentle smile he raised his glass to me. I knew then he had just died, and the next day my feeling was confirmed when I learned that Al had indeed passed at 10 p.m., Pacific Daylight Time.

NOTES

1. "I Wish I'd Been There," Peter Dyck, *Mennonite Historical Bulletin*, July 2000
2. *Johann "Hans" Ediger, 1775–1994*, C.T. Friesen, Houston: Author, 1994
3. Russia, Global Anabaptist Mennonite Encyclopedia Online, Accessed Apr. 24, 2009
4. *My Memoirs, David Paetkau, 1903–1972*
5. *Ibid.*
6. *Ibid.*
7. *Ibid.*
8. *Ibid.*
9. *Ibid.*
10. Hay River, Northwest Territories, and Great Slave Lake, Wikipedia Online Encyclopedia, accessed Jan. 19, 2009
11. "Hospital administrator tenders resignation," *The Peninsula Times*, May 27, 1964
12. Dr. Richard Alan Churchill Swan, oral history, Apr. 12, 2002, Sechelt Community Archives
13. "First war veteran led varied career," *The Peninsula Times*, June 9, 1971
14. Dr. W.N. McKee Notice, *Coast News*, Sept. 17, 1959
15. "MacIntyre to Hear Trade Board Kick," *Coast News*, Mar. 22, 1951; "Officials praise hospital brief," *Coast News*, Dec. 17, 1959
16. "Found," *Coast News*, Feb. 16, 1961
17. Aho, Aaro E. *Hills of Silver: The Yukon's Mighty Keno Hill Mine.* Harbour Publishing, Madeira Park, 2006, pages 151–162.
18. "Background on hospital," *Coast News*, Vol. 22, No. 46, Nov. 27, 1964; "Lloyd outlines case to trustees, wants old hospital retained," *Coast News*, Sept. 14, 1961
19. "Winter Hamlet Echoes Its Pioneer Beginnings," Andrew Scott, www.straight.com, Jan. 27, 2005
20. "Whopping hospital vote," *Coast News*, May 31, 1962
21. Dr. Richard Alan Churchill Swan, oral history, Apr. 12, 2002, Sechelt Community Archives
22. *The West Howe Sound Story*, Francis J. Van Den Wyngaert, Pegasus Press, 1980
23. *Ibid.*
24. "Youth lucky to be alive after plunge," *The Peninsula Times*, Sept. 3, 1975
25. *Coast News*, Jan. 22, 1969
26. "Vote approves hospital expansion," *Coast News*, Feb. 26, 1969
27. "St. Mary's Hospital emergency cases only rule as construction crawls on," *The Peninsula Times*, July 28, 1971, page 1; "Make-Shift," *The Peninsula Times*, Aug. 4, 1971
28. "Brummell freed," *Coast News*, May 30, 1971, page 1

29. See Accreditation Canada Website (www.accreditation-canada.ca) Accreditation Process

30. "Hospital receives full accreditation," *The Peninsula Times*, Nov. 13, 1974; "St. Mary's gains help from visiting experts," *The Peninsula Times*, Apr. 2, 1975; "St. Mary's moves from red to black," *Shopper-Press*, Apr. 7, 1976, page 10

31. "Hospital emergency," *Sunshine Shopper*, Mar. 18, 1975; "Hospital expansion plan outlined by administrator," *The Peninsula Times*, July 23, 1975

32. "St. Mary's moves from red to black," *Shopper-Press*, Apr. 7, 1976, page 10; "Resource society active," Hugh Duff, *Sunshine Shopper*, Mar. 11, 1975

33. "Doctors on emergency duty at St. Mary's," *The Peninsula Times*, Feb. 27, 1974

34. "Eric Paetkau of the Social Credit," interview by Leslie Yates, *The Peninsula Times*, Nov. 19, 1975, page A6

35. *Ibid.*

36. *Ibid.*

37. Interviews with local candidates, *Coast News*, Dec. 3, 1975, page 4; "Eric Paetkau of the Social Credit," interview by Leslie Yates, *The Peninsula Times*, Nov. 19, 1975, page A6

38. "Eric Paetkau of the Social Credit," interview by Leslie Yates, *The Peninsula Times*, Nov. 19, 1975, page A6

39. "Save our salmon project reports success," *Coast News*, Sept. 3, 1975, page 1; "Local salmon enhancement investigated," *The Peninsula Times*, Nov. 26, 1975, page B6

40. "Saving Eric," letter to the editor, *The Peninsula Times*, Nov. 19, 1975, page A4; "Good Doctors are Hard to Find," letter to the editor, *The Peninsula Times*, Dec. 3, 1975, page A4

41. "Rally fizzles into non-debate," *The Vancouver Sun*, Dec. 3, 1975, page 1

42. "All-candidates' meeting hears only 2 views—Socred, Liberal," *The Peninsula Times*, Dec. 10, 1975, page A2

43. "Lockstead a winner amid NDP losers," *The Peninsula Times*, Dec. 17, 1975, page 1

44. *Ibid.*

45. Dr. Richard Alan Churchill Swan, oral history, Apr. 12, 2002, Sechelt Community Archives

46. "North With Alan Swan," Sechelt Notes, Peggy Connor, *The Peninsula Times*, June 22, 1977, page A6

47. "Sechelt doctors' case presented on Pender Clinic support," Pender Harbour Ratepayers' Association, *Coast News*, Sept. 6, 1977

48. Somalia, Andrew Cockburn, *National Geographic* Magazine On-Line Extra, July 2002; Somalia People 1993, 1993 CIA World Factbook; www.countrystudies.us, accessed Apr. 17, 2009

49. "How the Culture of Aid Gave Us the Tragedy of Somalia," Michael Maren, *The Village Voice*, Jan. 19, 1993; Somalia, Andrew Cockburn, *National Geographic* Magazine On-Line Extra, July 2002

50. "How the Culture of Aid Gave us the Tragedy of Somalia," Michael Maren, *The Village Voice*, Jan. 19, 1993

51. Schistosmoiasis (Bilharzia) HealthLink, Medical College of Wisconsin, Apr 1, 2002

52. Republic of Tajikistan, Encyclopedia of the Nations, C2009-Advameg Inc. http://www.nationsencyclopedia.com/Asia-and-Oceania/Tajikistan-HISTORY.html

53. "Khujand," Encyclopaedia Britannica, 2009. Encyclopaedia Britannica Online Library Edition. 4 2009. http://library.eb.com/eb/article-9045353

54. Aral Sea, Address of the Chairman of the Executive Committee of the International Fund on the Aral Sea, Tebeki Altyev, Regional Report of the Central Asian States 2000, Sept. 2000

55. Jill Sampson, Wikipedia, the free encyclopedia, accessed Feb. 8, 2009

56. Foster, Lynn V., *A Brief History of Central America.* New York: Checkmark Books, 2007

57. Faith in Practice website, c2004

58. "Most board members are competent, report says," by Stewart Bell, *The Vancouver Sun*, Apr. 13, 1998, page A6

59. "Your Partners in Health," *The Reporter*, Oct. 17, 1999, page 27

60. "Forty-two years," Keith Bradford, *Coast Reporter*, Apr. 14, 2002, page A16

61. "The Class of 1989 and physician supply in Canada," Eva Ryten, BS ocSc, DipPol; A. Dianne Thurber, BSc, MA; Lynda Buske, BSc. 1998 *Canadian Medical Association Journal*, 1998

62. Task Force on Physician Supply in Canada, Lorne Tyrell and Dale Dauphinee on behalf of the Canadian Medical Forum Task Force, co-chaired by Dr. Hugh Scully, Pres CMA and Dr. Lorne Tyrrell, Pres of ACMC, Nov. 22, 1999

63. "Specialists' thinning ranks," Julia Cyboran, *National Review of Medicine*, Vol 3 No 5, Mar. 15, 2006

64. "Forty-two years," Keith Bradford, *Coast Reporter*, Apr. 14, 2002, page A16